REBRANDED

Transforming the Tattoo Nightmares in Your Mind

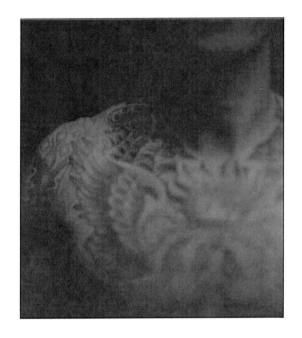

Pastor Dave Minton

With Contribution by Trisha Ferguson

Creative Force Press

Creative Force Press

Rebranded
© 2014 by Dave Minton
With contribution by Trisha Ferguson
www.go2ccc.org

This title is also available as an eBook. Visit
www.CreativeForcePress.com/titles for more information.

Published by Creative Force Press
4704 Pacific Ave, Suite C, Lacey, WA 98503
www.CreativeForcePress.com

ISBN: 978-1-939989-11-6

Printed in the USA - For worldwide distribution

Dave Minton has led his own family and church by learning to be led by the Holy Spirit. His ministry has grown through some of life's greatest challenges. He is one of those men we can follow by example.

Casey Treat, Author & Senior Pastor of Christian Faith Center, Federal Way, WA

CONTENTS

 INTRODUCTION

What is a tattoo nightmare? It's an unwanted mark stamped on you, because of a bad decision: having something written on your body that you regret, resulting in embarrassment and shame. It's a branding, and often painful.

In life, the tender environment of our spiritual hearts can quickly become covered with painful tattoos; tattoos of rejection, injustices, abuse, neglect, vanity, selfishness, pain, and shame.

Despite these seemingly permanent, embarrassing inscriptions, God is the Master of transformation; a skilled Artist ready to redesign every negative mark into something beautiful, refreshing to your soul, and for His purposes.

You do not need to live any longer with the wounds, shame, and tattoos of regret and betrayal. You do not need to live any longer trying to hide your embarrassing heart tattoos from others.

As you read, if you will trust Him today, He will be faithful and just to forgive your sins and start a process of redesigning and complete transformation in your heart and mind.

1

HIDDEN SHAME

Unwanted heart tattoos seem to come easily. Because of bad decisions, our spiritual hearts and minds retain undesirable marks that cause us regret, embarrassment, and shame. Other people harming us causes some of these damaging tattoos. Sometimes we choose to tattoo ourselves.

It's a tattoo received during a drunken binge, and the next morning you say, "Oh, my God, how did that get there? I don't want it there anymore!"

Maybe it's the name of a person that you thought you'd love forever inscribed on your arm, only to find out that they betrayed you, leaving an emotional wound. Now you're stuck looking at that name all the time; a constant reminder of the pain they inflicted upon your heart.

Maybe it's a tattoo you got at a stage in your life when you thought it would be really cool. Then, you got married or you started having children, or you showed it to your parents, and all of a sudden you realized that it really wasn't so cool after all. You grew out of that season of your life and you wish it wasn't there anymore.

These are tattoo nightmares. With these kind of tattoos, we become desperate to cover them up. We're ashamed of them and start wearing long-sleeved shirts when it's 100 degrees outside. We'll do odd things to try not to expose ourselves. It's something we regret and we're ashamed of, and we begin the quest to cover it up.

This message is not to debate whether or not getting a tattoo is right or wrong. Some of my close relationships have tattoos. This is not about being against tattoos. It is about something much deeper.

I love the TV show *Tattoo Nightmares*. This show features real people who have tattoos they regret getting, they're really ashamed of, and feel embarrassed about. A new tattoo artist will go to work on the embarrassing tattoo, and when he's done with it, it's totally transformed. Suddenly, it becomes something they're proud of, something they want to show off, and something they want to tell everybody about.

That's exactly what God wants to do with our lives. He wants to take the places of our lives—the parts of our lives with regret, the places we're ashamed of, the parts of our lives that are embarrassing to us—and go to work as the Master Artist, turning those broken parts into something we're truly proud and unashamed of.

With God, we're not talking about physical tattoos; it's deeper. He works on the kind of tattoos that get on our souls, on our minds, and into our hearts.

Years ago, Norman Vincent Peale, author of *The Power of Positive Thinking,* was walking through the streets of Hong Kong and sees a tattoo shop. He paused as he noticed the various pictures and wording in the window of examples of what you can have tattooed on your body; pictures like the flag, an anchor, mermaids, etc.

He reads one that says "Born to Lose." He thought to himself, *people wouldn't really put that on their body, would they?* He went inside and asked the tattoo artist, "Does anybody really get that phrase put on their body?" The artist says, "Of course they do." Dr. Peale said, "I cannot believe that anyone would put that phrase on their body." The artist began to tap his forehead and said, "Before tattoo on body, tattoo on mind."

Some people have been tattooed with cruel words that have stamped their heart. Even if you don't have a physical tattoo declaring the words, you might believe that you were born to lose. You might believe you were born to be mistreated. You might believe you were born to be addicted. You might believe you were born to be rejected. Or, perhaps a person at work tattooed something on your reputation that has become a nightmare in your life. Perhaps you've suffered a betrayal that has affected the way you conduct yourself in subsequent relationships.

Perhaps you've experienced some kind of betrayal or someone victimized you. It might be abuse at the hand of a parent or another adult who abused you — or sexually abused you—and somehow put that mark on you. You might be thinking you deserved it or that it was your fault. Sometimes when bad things happen to us, we internalize it and start to think we brought it on ourselves.

Maybe you lost someone who died before their natural time. When we bury someone after a good long life, there's a sense of satisfaction. But, when a parent buries their child, something about that feels very wrong.

There's also something not right about burying a spouse. I met someone who had been married forty years and had just lost their spouse. They were struggling, trying to work through this new season of their life. That loss became been tattooed on them. It's hard to live in the present and enjoy life today when your heart is tattooed with a loss.

A 'loss' tattoo is like trying to pour water into a cup with a hole in it. It won't hold anything because you're so consumed with grief and all the implications of that loss.

The nightmare we struggle with could be something someone else did to us or something we did to ourselves. Have you ever noticed the incredible capacity we have to seriously mess up something really good? We get a good job...and mess it up. We get a good relationship...and mess it up. We get a great opportunity and mess it up, too. All these regrets become tattooed onto our hearts.

You're not alone when it comes to messing things up. In fact, messing up something good was part of the original sin.

Remember the story of Adam and Eve in the Garden of Eden? Imagine this: Adam and Eve were not happy with their life, as-is. They're in relationship with God, they're living in a lush garden, they've got an incredible personal life, and yet they're not content walking in the garden visiting with God. The Bible said it was pride — the lust of the flesh, the lust of the eye and the pride of life — that made them dissatisfied with who they were.

In an attempt to become somebody they were not (God), it caused them to have a scar they would live with the rest of their lives. The Bible says they were created — both the man and the woman, the man and his wife — naked and they were not ashamed. But after trying to be somebody they weren't, they became ashamed. Pride is about trying to be somebody we're not, trying to measure up, trying to fit in, trying to be better than who we are.

Some of us are trying to have something better, and in many cases that is a good thing. I believe in going to the next level, and I believe in the promises of God. He offers us a better life, but I don't believe that a better life comes at the expense of the present life. That's why a lot of people don't enjoy where they are, now. They think happiness is a destination. Trust me, happiness is not a destination: happiness is in the journey.

It's a statistical fact that when most people leave their

first marriage, after a while they forget about what went wrong; the pain, resentment, regret, disappointment, and hurt. They end up longing for what they missed. If they had do-overs, they would stay in their first marriage.

We have an incredible ability to do things to ourselves that cause a lot of regrets. That's exactly what Adam and Eve did. They were in paradise, naked and not ashamed until they agreed to sin. God said, "Adam, where are you?" It's not like He didn't know where Adam was. He wasn't looking under bushes for him, "Oh Adam, where are you?" He knew exactly where he was, but was trying to pull him out of hiding. "Adam, where are you? Where are you? Where are you?"

Adam said, "I hid myself." When you go from not being ashamed to being ashamed, you hide...maybe in a ditch. Maybe you hide in an affair. Maybe you hide in a fantasy life. Maybe you hide in something that's keeping your life stuck. You're hiding in these things and you're trying to cover up – you're ashamed, and you want to cover up your embarrassing tattoo. This is exactly when God wants to enter in as an Artist.

God said, "Adam, where are you?" And Adam said, "I hid myself because I was naked. I was afraid." Then God said, "Who told you that you were naked? I didn't put that on you." You know the story. Did he stand up like a man and own his err? No! Not a chance! "It's *your* fault, God, because you gave me the woman, and she's the one who made me do it." Adam blamed God and his wife.

You may be in a mindset of blaming God. Instead of taking responsibility and saying, "In my foolishness and in my drunkenness and in my inappropriateness and in my immaturity, I got a tattoo on me that I now regret," blame is easier. Somehow, it's not your fault because you were talked into it. "It's got to be Your fault, God, because You weren't there for me and You didn't stop me. It's got to be Your fault because You're God and I'm not."

We have all these reactions to cover up and hide our bad decisions. We don't want to take ownership for these tattoos. Whether it's something that somebody's done to us or something we do to ourselves (or a combination of both), God wants to be the healer of heart wounds that scar our lives. He wants to be the healer of the wounds that leave an imprint; that leave a mark on our minds.

WHO CARES ABOUT YOUR PAST?

Let me tell you, you *do not have to* live in the shame of your past. You do not have to be stuck in the loss of your past. You do not have to be branded by past failures. God wants to step in and be the Master Tattoo Artist in your life.

In Genesis chapter 1 — in the story of Creation — it talks about how the earth was without form and void. Envision that: the earth was without form and void. Void is a Hebrew word that means a *formless, chaotic mess*. It's without structure, full of craziness, a desolate wasteland without purpose. Could this be describing your life? The ingredients of void soup might be barrenness, emptiness, lost-ness, incompleteness, purposeless, loneliness, and wastefulness.

This was the earth, until God moved in. The Spirit of God was hovering, watching over, swaying, and moving over the face of the water. "And God said, 'Let there be light.'" I want you to imagine when God speaks, it's like the needle when a tattoo artist begins to tap into your flesh. When God began to poke into that void, into that waste place, He began to poke into the place of craziness and chaos. "Let there be light, and there was light."

It's amazing that when God says something, it shows up. God takes pride in His work. If you've ever seen the tattoo show, the premise of it is bringing in extreme, nightmare tattoo cases; people with really awful tattoo mistakes and regrets. The drama of it is whether or not the artist can fix. They always say, "That's really bad. I don't know if we can fix it. It's really awful. I'd hate to have that on my body. I'm stressed out about trying to fix their problem." Then, they do something transformational, and the artist is proud of it. "I'm so proud of what I just did!"

I don't care how ashamed you are, I don't care how addicted you are, I don't care how grieved you are, I don't care how lost you are, I don't care what a waste you've been, and I don't care how huge of a mess you've made. I'm telling you this:

When God is done with you, He's going to say, "That's good. I did a good job. You may not know it, but I did a good job. I'm really proud of My work."

It's called *redemption*: it's what God does. He is the Redeemer of broken lives. He's the Redeemer of lost dreams. He is the Redeemer. God divided the light from the darkness. He separated those things, and He will separate them within you.

God is trying to add a new chapter to your life. He says to your spirit, *this was the dark part of your life, but the dark part of your life is not the present part, nor shall it be your future part. I'm separating your past from your present. I'm separating your past from your future.* You may be dealing with difficult times. I want you to know that God wants to come in as an incredible Tattoo Artist and bring healing to that area of your life.

There is an amazing couple in our church family who have been clean and sober and serving God for over thirty years now. This is their testimony:

Wife: "I grew up in a very dysfunctional family. My mother was an addict and she also struggled with mental issues. Life was very unpredictable. At fifteen I had attempted suicide. I found ways to cope by isolating myself. I ended up with an unplanned pregnancy. At that point I bottomed out, I just felt hopeless. At night I started to cry out to God and ask Him for help. Then I accepted Jesus as my personal Savior. I learned that He valued my life. I began my journey; my life started to blossom in the Lord. Now every area of my life is for His purpose and to serve Him. I'm living the dream, I'm living this blessed life, because I'm submitted to Christ. That is my most important relationship, because out of that relationship I found my purpose; I found my value. I thank God that now I can take that value and express it through Celebrate Recovery, and let other people know that God loves them! God has transformed my nightmares into dreams, and a future filled with hope."

Husband: "As for me, I was the youngest of four. My father was a career soldier. I was molested by a neighbor boy. There was a lot of pain. My dad drank. When I started experimenting with drugs, life started to go even crazier. Soon after that, I got involved with a drugstore robbery. The law didn't matter, the drugs were overpowering. I was listening to the radio one night and I heard a spiritual invitation. I knew about God but I didn't know a personal Savior and that His name was Jesus Christ. Jesus has given me hope. God has transformed my nightmares into dreams."

If God will do that for this couple, God will do that for you. Praise the Lord!

The Bible says that the Spirit of God was hovering over the face of the earth; hovering over what was dark, what was void, what was craziness, looking for the opportunity to penetrate into that void. Now, have you ever noticed that we usually have to get into a broken place before God can penetrate?

He has always been there, but we have to come to a place where we drop our guard. Maybe we have to go to jail. Maybe we're in the middle of a divorce. Maybe we're in the middle of a disease that doctors are saying there's no cure for. Something unexpected comes into our life, and all of a sudden there's an open opportunity where God says, "Now I can work." He's been hovering, watching over, swaying over, and the open door comes. And in that open door, God wants to penetrate into your heart. In those moments, the Spirit of God wants to *leave a mark on your soul*. In other words, He wants to tattoo you with blessing. The calling of God wants to mark your soul with something of heaven.

Listen to what God is saying to us in Hebrews 8:10. The Message version says:

"I'm writing out the plan in them. Carving it on the lining of their heart. I will be their God and they will be my people."

Do you hear what God is saying to you? He doesn't care what your past has been. He wants to carve a message on your heart, that you belong to Him.

I'll be a Father to you, I'll be a protector of you, I'll watch over you, and I'll provide for you. I want to tattoo that message of hope and love so that you can trust in Me. You can rely on Me, you can depend on Me, and I'll be there for you.

FOREVER IS CALLING

When God marks us with this sense of calling, it is *forever*. It begins to create a Genesis moment in our life that begins a separation: our past from our future, the moment that He penetrates our life.

If you know and study scripture, and you notice the people in the Bible who God called, you know there was a drastic difference between their past, the moment of their calling, and their future. God's call changed the direction of their lives. It was a divine crossroads; the **Y** in the road that forever altered their course. Let's discuss a few of these saints.

Moses was a murderer. After killing a slave driver, the Egyptians wanted to arrest him for murder. He was Jewish, but wasn't part of Jewish culture – he grew up in the Egyptian palace. He had an identity crisis: he didn't know who he was or where he fit.

After fleeing the country, he ended up on the backside of the wilderness living in a waste place. The Spirit of God began to speak to him. He's a murderer, but God says, "I need you to be my deliverer. I need you to be my leader." The calling of God left a mark on his heart.

His life did a 180-degree shift.

Joseph, the Bible says, was betrayed by his brothers who sold him into slavery. But, even while he was in slavery he still prospered. How is it possible to prosper while in slavery? When God is with you, it is possible. However, while he's prospering as a slave in Potiphar's house and being given great responsibility, Potiphar's wife tried to get him to commit adultery, and he rejected her. He said, "I can't do that against my master in his household." So, being slighted, she accused him of rape and he's unjustly thrown into prison. The Bible says, in prison he even prospered!

How do you prosper in prison, exactly? Does that look like having more cigarettes than anybody else? Does he have the best cell? The Bible says he's prospering in prison, but our modern ideas of prosperity pop into our minds. Houses and cars? Bank accounts? I don't know what pops into your mind when you read the word *prosperity* in scripture, but the Bible says he prospered while in prison. But the reality is he's locked up; he's in a dank dungeon...he doesn't have freedom.

The story goes on to say that Pharaoh, the king of Egypt himself, called Joseph out to seek his wisdom, and overnight he went from rags to riches. The Bible says Pharaoh put fine clothes on him and a gold chain. Pharaoh had him ride in the second, fancy chariot. He suddenly became extremely wealthy with favor and possessions.

Here's what I'm really trying to say: Joseph had

something in his heart that was *not* shaped by his dire circumstances. Even though from the outside it all looked bad, God said, "I'll bless him anyway because that boy's got a different tattoo on his heart. That boy's going to prosper." God was with him.

You might be in a situation where you're being victimized, but the call of God, whether you see it today or not, is changing the direction and the course of your life. If you let Him continue working on the lining of your heart, on the inner person of your spirit, and on the inner person of your being, your relationship with Him will change the direction of your life.

If you always look for external leadership from the outside, you're going to miss the inner direction of God.

Gideon argued with God. One day the Angel of the Lord shows up and tells Gideon he will deliver Israel from Midianite oppression. He responds in unbelief, "You're crazy." He begins to argue while he's hiding, sneaking out to collect a little bit of food while the Midianites aren't looking. While he's hiding, God is talking to him. This is Gideon's response starting at Judges 6:15:

"O my Lord, O my God," this is frustrating. "How can I save Israel?" What he says next is remarkable. "Indeed my clan, Manasseh, is the weakest tribe of all the tribes of Israel, and I am the weakest in my father's house." Our tribe is the weakest tribe, and my family is the weakest family in the weakest tribe, and I happen to be the weakest member in the weakest family of the weakest tribe. He's basically telling God He's got the wrong guy. Do you ever feel like that?

When someone gets a tattoo, the artist wants them to sit still for a moment before he or she begins tattooing. Sometimes, when God is trying to get started working, He says, "Will you just sit still for a minute, so I can get started? Stop with the excuses, stop with the complaining, stop with the whining, and let Me just get started. Let me get My message into your heart."

God's call on your life leaves a mark, and that mark is what separates your past from your present, what separates your past from your future. God wants today to be the first day of the rest of your life. God is trying to put a mark on you through His Word; through His Spirit. He's hovering over your mess, He's hovering over your craziness, He's hovering over your chaos, He's hovering over your waste places, He's hovering over your shame, He's hovering over your regrets, and He's hovering over your hurt. He's saying, *will you give Me a place where I can penetrate? Will you give Me an opening where I can just speak to your heart? Will you let My Word become a tattoo on your heart and mind? I will be your God.*

You may have been rejected by people, but I have not rejected you. You may have been rejected by your children — your own children — but I have not rejected you. You may have been betrayed by people that should have treated you better. But I will watch over you, I will be there for you.

Will you let Me leave My mark on your heart that will

forever change the next season of your life?

The Spirit of God, the calling of God, wants to create in your life a new history.

In 2 Corinthians 5:17, it says, "If anyone be in Christ..." Are you in Christ? That means you've put your faith in God. You've allowed God to put His mark on your heart. That's called being born again and becoming a new creation – that is, "old things have passed away." Look at the new! When the old tattoo is gone, let's take a good look at the new thing He is doing in our lives. We keep wanting to remind Him of the old tattoo. He says, *look, a new season, a new day, and a new image has come.*

God wants to create a new history in your life. It does not mean He wants to re-write the old history. It doesn't mean He wants you to deny the old history, either.

If you've been violated, you've been violated. Don't try to suppress that truth or pretend it never happened. A lot of addiction and physical illness comes from trying to suppress pain in our lives. God's not talking about suppressing your old history; He's talking about creating a new history. If you understand this, it's going to change your life. It's not about re-writing the old, or denying the old; it's creating something new.

How do we do that? Do something today so that when tomorrow comes, it becomes yesterday's memories. You do something today! If God has left a mark, then let that mark start taking effect. What you do today will become tomorrow's memories of yesterday.

Most people are stuck in something that happened five, ten or even fifteen years ago, and that's where they still live. And whatever injustice, loss or offense happened to them, the mark of that event—not the mark of God, some other negative mark left on them—is what they live today, because it affects their memories of yesterday.

With You, For You, or Against You?

Isn't it great to be a follower of Christ? Isn't it exciting what God can do? How He can rescue us? We don't deserve to have blessed lives, but I'm grateful for it! It's all because of His goodness, not because of ours.

A newer church member told me about a tattoo he wouldn't show me because he was so embarrassed about it. He got it from a guy who had just bought his equipment. It was cheap. The tattoo ended up being so bad he wouldn't let anyone see it. He took my advice, and his brother did a makeover of it. Afterward, he showed it to me. What a great job! He tried to point out the mistakes his brother covered up, but it was such an amazing transformation that I couldn't see the previous mess ups.

His tattoo nightmare has turned into something he loves now. Even more interesting was him trying to show me what was underneath, but I couldn't see it any more.

How many know that when you try to see past the blood of Jesus into your old life, you just can't see it anymore. Jesus has the ability to take those places in our life that we're ashamed of, or embarrassed of, or our regrets, and has the ability as an Artist to change and redeem those things into a life of grace. It's not about who you are but about who He is, and the ability of what He can do in your life.

One of the greatest tattoo nightmares we have to overcome is the tattoo of betrayal, abuse, and victimization. Every one of us will deal with betrayal at some point throughout the course of our lives. We all experience it to some degree.

Betrayal comes from relationships that you least expect it to; from relationships that you trust or rely on most.

We have a variety of relationship types: friends, family, acquaintances, co-workers, spouses, and such. Some of these relationships are with people who are *with* us. They are on our side helping us accomplish our goals. Then there are people who are *for* us; they're not really *with* us, but they're certainly not against us. They're for us. Those people say, "You go! You make it happen; that's awesome, keep me posted." Then, you have the people who want something from you. It might be a family member, and the only time they come around is when they want something. In the relationship, they just use you. People even do this with God, in a way, when they only come to church when they need a miracle.

Then, there are people who are against you. It's very clear that you don't like each other. "You don't like me.

We're not going to do business together. You feel it's your calling to persecute me. I get it...you're against me."

The worst betrayal comes when it's a *with you* person who uses you and ends up against you. You think, *what just happened?* And you have this incredible wound on your soul. You get tattooed in the heart. It never comes at a good time. If you're a business person, the business is starting to take off, and you have an employee that goes sideways on you, or a partner that betrays you. Maybe you're working on a project at work. You have a brilliant idea, and you share it with the supervisor. The supervisor implements and takes credit for your idea. And you think, *what just happened?*

Or your spouse is sleeping in somebody else's bed, and you feel incredibly violated. You find out what's happening, and you thought the marriage was strong. Maybe you're engaged and looking forward to marriage. Friends or relatives reveal secrets and say, "Did you hear what they are doing with who?" You're thinking, *what just happened? I thought we had a future.*

Can anybody related to what I'm talking about?

Maybe you're a student and you shared something private, revealing vulnerable areas of yourself and you felt you could trust that person...only to find they posted your sensitive information on Twitter, Facebook and everywhere else. You feel so violated because you thought you had the confidence of a friend and found out they used you. We all experience betrayal in our lives.

Betrayal is a tattoo the enemy wants to put on you. Please understand this: you didn't deserve your betrayal, but the enemy wants you to be hurt *and* tattooed by it forever.

Often, that tattoo attempt comes because there's favor on your life. But it sours you, and you shift from feeling special and that God is with you, to feeling that God has rejected you. This is a lie, but that mark on you can negatively change the course and direction of your life.

Here's what you have to understand: everyone will experience some degree of betrayal. Some experience horrific betrayal; violence, rape, abuse, and very serious victimization. You may be reading this and that has been your experience. If so, I pray that the God of Grace erases that tattoo on you, and He transforms it into a place of redemption instead.

Maybe you had a spouse that badly betrayed you, when you thought you had their confidence. Maybe you supported them through school and you worked. Then by the time they got their degree, they ran off with somebody else, and left you with a mess. Trespasses like that happen all the time. They cause a wound in you.

When you've been betrayed, be cautious. You have been victimized, but if you don't let God heal you, it's very possible for *you* to become the victimizer. In other words, hurtful people come from hurt people.

Offensive people come from being offended. Abusers come from being abused.

If you and I were to go and interview any inmate in a jail, you could ask them to tell you two stories:

1. What did you do that got you here?
2. What happened to you that caused you to do that?

If they told you what they did that got them there, you'd be very angry at them. You'd think *they deserve this jail cell for life*. If they told you the second story — what happened to them that got them there — then you might weep over them. We know that sexual abusers come from the sexually abused. We know that people who hit people come from people who have been hit by people.

There are two stories in our lives. There's the story of the person who was victimized and betrayed, who, if they don't get it healed, become the victimizer and the betrayer. It's important that we recognize this issue in our lives and allow God to visit us there. Or, we can keep and live with a mark on our soul that we are ashamed of and embarrassed by.

As an example, let's look at the story of the children of Israel. God came to them and told them He was going to deliver them from their slavery in Egypt. They were in bondage for 450 years. What is the reason they were in bondage? Because there was favor on their lives. The reason the Egyptians abused them was because they were being fruitful; their population was increasing. I hope you catch the significance of this.

Maybe you're in a place today in your life that is really hard, and you're able to complain about people who have it better. But should your life get better, guess what you have to get ready for? People who complain about you. The problems you have today should they be solved, may not be the problems you have tomorrow.

As slaves, the children of Israel are being oppressed and victimized on a daily basis. God hears their groaning, and He sends Moses to be their leader, their answer. Take a look at this story in Exodus chapter 6. God tells Moses to tell the people that God has heard their groaning, and has seen their bondage to the Egyptians. "I have remembered my covenant," God says, "therefore I say to the children of Israel, I am the Lord." This is not a phrase, this is a statement: *I am the Lord*.

Watch how many times He makes promises, saying, "I WILL bring you out from under the burden of the Egyptians. I WILL rescue you from their bondage. I WILL redeem you with an outstretched arm and with great judgment. I WILL take you as my people, and I WILL be your God." He goes on to say, "Then you shall know that I am the Lord your God who brings you out from under the burden of the Egyptians." I WILL bring you into the land which I swore to give Abraham, Isaac and Jacob. I WILL give it to you as an inheritance. I WILL. You will be my people. And he closes with "I AM THE LORD."

There are seven I WILL promises in total. In verse 9, Moses spoke them to the children of Israel, and it says, "BUT THEY DID NOT HEAR MOSES, because of anguish of spirit and cruel bondage." The tattoo of their abuse and slavery, the tattoo of their victimization, the tattoo of their betrayal, cut them so severely it impacted their ability to hear and receive what God had for them. That word, *anguish of spirit* literally means *shortness of soul*.

You and I can have a small soul or a big soul; a small heart or a big heart. The Bible says that anguish of soul (shortness of soul) refers to something being cut off; cut off, small or little. Something's growth gets cut off before reaching maturity.

Abuse often happens in the heart of a child before they become mature. How many know that if abuse happened to a child, had they been mature, they may not have allowed that abuse to happen? But the abuse happened in a season of vulnerability, and it refers to cutting them short, preventing and stunting them from maturing into what God has planned.

Abuse and betrayal have the ability to stunt our growth. It shortens and cuts off our ability to hear from God. It cuts off our ability to see what God has for us. It cuts off our ability to relate well and seek better relationships. Inhumane treatment was put upon the children of Israel.

Remember, this is why God steps in. God says, *I see what is happening to you, I hear your groaning, and I see your sorrows. I'm going to step in. I'm going to get involved with you. I'm going to help. I will rescue you. I will redeem you. I will be your God. I will pick you up. I will bring you in. I will do this thing. I am the Lord.*

BITTER WALLS

When we have betrayals in our lives, the deep wounds cause us to start putting up *I won't trust people again* walls in our hearts. *I won't love somebody, because if I do love somebody, they might love me back. If they love me back, I know how this plays out. They leave me. They lie to me. They cheat on me. They use me. People who are supposed to be for me, I often find out are against me, because they end up using me. So, I'm just going to build some walls to keep others out. I'm going to isolate and insulate myself from people. I'll just get myself a pet.*

Pets are loyal, right? I'm not against pets, but I am against isolation. Please ask yourself this: Do I have a pet because I don't want a relationship? And if I don't want a relationship, is it because I got wounded? Am I afraid of being rejected again? *Being the cat lady sounds better!*

We build walls that isolate us to shut people out. We don't want people to hurt us anymore. But the walls that shut hurtful people out are the same walls that shut helpful people out. The same walls we hide within are the same walls that keep hurt and pain in. When you build walls you find yourself in a gloomy pit.

Again, the story of Joseph in the Bible is a great example of this. When Joseph was betrayed by his brothers, they betrayed him and literally threw him in a pit. The Bible says there was no water in the pit, but that doesn't mean that the pit was empty. When we get in this pit, we see that it's full of things like jealousy, bitterness, hatred, envy, sorrow, and grief. All of those things fuel betrayal and keep it alive. As long as your heart is full of these things, and you don't let God heal it, you begin to have pity parties.

I'm not trying to minimize the injustice inflicted upon someone who has been horrifically abused. I don't want to minimize your pain. But please hear me. You getting past your pain is crucial, otherwise if you get in the pit and start having pity parties, you'll become pitiful. Have you ever seen someone have a healthy relationship or rewarding relationship that is constantly struggling with bitterness in their lives? It just doesn't happen.

What if a person becomes bitter toward the government? Even that kind of bitterness can creep into affecting good relationships. If I'm bitter at my boss, it's hard to contain the root of bitterness there, too. Bitterness is something that grows up and produces fruit in our lives. I hope you understand this. When we try to contain bitterness within walls and say, "I don't like those people. I don't like that group of people," we're on our way to becoming the victimizer and the betrayer. Why? Because something is growing inside. It was marked on us; something evil, ungodly, and unrighteous.

We have to take responsibility when we get in the betrayal pit, because betrayal becomes internalized. Remember the story of when God's people were at the Red Sea, and they said, "Why did you bring us out here? The Lord hates us. And there's no water." And then Moses gets water out of the rock. "Why did we stop out here? We liked it better in Egypt." And God rains down manna (bread) from heaven. "We're sick of this manna and there's no bread and there's no meat." Then the Bible says they got so much meat they were choking on it.

Every time a problem came up, it was God's fault because God hated them. Every time adversity came up, they'd say, "Why'd You do this, God? Why'd You let me down, God? Why are You doing this to me? It's because the Lord hates us!" This was years after they were denied going into the Promised Land.

Moses said to them, "You complain, you complain in your tents that the Lord hates us." Remember, God said, "I saw your sorrow. I saw the way you were being treated. I saw what the Egyptians were doing to you. I saw your groaning. I saw your sorrow. I had mercy on you. I sent you a deliverer named Moses. I am your God. I will do it. I promise I'll be there for you. I won't leave you. I won't forsake you. I am the Lord. That's who I am." The people still respond, "You hate us!" He cannot win with their mindsets!

Realize that you are the gatekeeper of your thought life. You are the gatekeeper of the thoughts allowed in your head. God gives you His thoughts so He can give you a new life. So, when we get in a pit and start internalizing the pain, we internalize the wound, and it can go global and become a mentality. It's not the mentality of the redeemed: it's the mentality of the shamed. It's the mentality of the rejected. It's the mentality of the defeated. It's the mentality of the wounded. Again, I'm not trying to put anyone down. But, here's what I'm saying: everybody has a mentality, a mindset. Everybody has a way in which they interpret life. Everybody has a filter they see life through.

A mom and dad can come home and see their ten year old in the kitchen with a mess everywhere. He made soup all by himself, and he's got dishes everywhere, soup spilled all over the place, and things out of order. Mom freaks out. "Look at the mess you made!" Dad says, "This is awesome! Leave him alone, he's growing up!" They both *see* the same thing, but both interpret it very differently.

Each of us has a perception of how to interpret life. The problem comes when you don't realize what your perception is. Do you know your mentality about money? Do you know your mentality about relationships? Do you know your mentality about your God? Do you know your mentality about your self-image and your self-worth?

Listen to the children of Israel's mentality: they're on the verge of entering the Promised Land, and send twelve spies to secretly check it out. The twelve spies come back, and they give this report (Numbers 13): "We saw giants in the land. We saw giants, and we are like grasshoppers in our own sight! We saw giants. We saw us. Giants...big giants. Us small. Giants. Grasshoppers. Giants. Grasshoppers. We saw giants, and they saw us in their sight!"

When you internalize a belief system, you'll start projecting that belief system onto others and become convinced in your heart that's how others see you. If you can grasp what I am saying, it could set you free right now.

Many of us are not aware of our own mentality. We take our mentality and project it onto others. You'll meet someone new, and if you struggle with rejection, you'll automatically think they don't want to know you. How do you know what they think? *Because they did this, or they did that. I saw it in their eyes. They think they're better than me.* You make up evidence to perpetuate your skewed mindset. You don't *feel* like you belong. *They think they're better than me. I've seen the clothes they wear. I've seen the car they drive.* We will start projecting onto them the reflection we see of ourselves.

When I was a young pastor, I had a problem with paying attention. My mind is constantly planning, and I had difficulty being present in-the-moment. So, I'd be walking through church, ignoring people, moving on to my next thing, walking right by people. That really created a lot of problems for me. Even to this day I can be in a conversation with somebody and I'll leave the room; not physically, but mentality. Then I'll come back and think, how long was I gone? When my kids were little, I'd be talking to them and get tired of talking...I'd just slow down and stop. "DAD!" *Oh, yeah, how long was I gone?* I may be the only one who has this issue. Focusing is difficult for me!

I started hearing comments from people. *You don't like me. What do you mean, I don't like you? Why would you say that? You didn't say hi to me. You walked by me. You said hello to somebody else, but you didn't say hi to me.* I heard this so many times as a young pastor. It was creating a lot of issues for me. I probably heard that comment at least fifty times. At least a dozen times I've had to say to my congregation, "Repeat after me. Pastor Dave loves me." And then I've said, "Now look at me. Trust me. I stepped out in faith. I'm here giving my life and devotion so that somebody like you can win in life. I'm praying. I'm preparing to teach you each week. I'm trying to do the very best I can."

I'm not saying my behavior is right. It is bad behavior I've worked diligently to improve. But, I pray that people will look at the totality of my life and not just at the moment I didn't say hi. Please don't internalize other people's lack of people skills as a sense of rejection towards you.

Everyone has a mentality. The spies said they were like grasshoppers...*and people like us don't live in that land. People like us can't win those battles. People like us don't have that kind of favor on our lives.* Their mentality sabotaged their lives.

When you're in a pit having pitiful pity parties, you start inviting people in, because no one wants to have a party by themselves, right? Your pit relationships are going to be with people who hate what you hate and are against what you're against. You choose people who hurt like you hurt; who are wounded like you're wounded. They share your perspective. Healthy people aren't invited because they're pity-party poopers.

Here's a thought. For those of you who are late to worship on Sunday mornings, do you struggle with complaining in your life? All the children of Israel were complaining against Moses; complaining against the answer to their woes. At first, Moses said to God, "I don't want to go, find somebody else. I don't like myself. I can't even talk." Remember Moses? Moses had his own issues. Somebody put a tattoo on him. Thankfully Moses ends up saying yes to God's call, and he becomes part of freedom's answer. And the people are complaining against the answer!

Here's a thought for us. Could we be complaining against the answer God has given us in our lives?

- How many of us might be complaining against the spouse that we asked God to give us?
- How many might be complaining against the job we asked God to give us?
- How many might be complaining against the children that we asked God to give us?
- How many might be complaining against the ministry that we asked God to give us?

We have this incredible capacity to take a good thing and begin to complain about it. Because we don't have right thinking about it, we will sabotage our life and get victimized. We don't even see it coming.

So, back to the Bible story. The people are all complaining against Moses and against Aaron. "Oh, if only we had died in the land of Egypt. If only we had died in the wilderness. WHY? WHY? Why did God bring us out here?" They complained regardless of who they followed. That's how they acted when the Egyptians beat them. That's how they acted even when God was good to them.

Now they question God's motives. "Here's what we'll do," they said. "Let's return to Egypt." You can always tell a person's true colors when the old tattoos start coming back out. They start moving from the front to the back. They start not showing up regularly. They say things like, "Let's select a leader and return to Egypt." They start going back.

Some are on a journey to get out of an addiction ditch through attending Celebrate Recovery. People trying to escape addiction have minds that caught *This is exhausting, I'm weary. I don't feel like I fit here. I don't feel like I belong. I don't know how to be sober. I don't know how to live without drama. I don't know how to live without an adrenalin rush in my life. I just need to find me a leader and go back to crazy! I just want to go back to crazy – it's familiar. I want to go back to abuse.* Do you understand? They're that close to the Promised Land! They are *that* close!

There could be miracle after miracle happening all

around you, but a miracle will not change your belief system. You don't need a new miracle, you need a new thought tattooed on your heart by the Spirit of God that will cause you to change the way you approach life. Then you'll have a renewed mind and see miracles in abundance.

THE PIT OF BETRAYAL

You may be a mere thought away from a life of miracles. But, if your belief system doesn't change, it doesn't matter how many miracles God does.

I quit looking for miracles a long time ago. Instead, I started looking for thoughts. I'm always on the lookout for the thought that will get me where I need to go. *Your thoughts are higher than my thoughts, Lord, and Your ways are higher than my ways, and the heavens are higher than the earth. Your thoughts are higher than my thoughts.* I must have higher thoughts and higher ways, and those only come from God. God is never afraid. He's never insecure. He's never weak in His thoughts.

Here's a new, God thought: you and I are not going back. You and I are going to have God put a tattoo on our hearts and do a new work in our lives. Today is your day! Today is a new beginning. The word of God is going to get through today. It's time for you to break out of your pit so your future can be bright.

It is time! It is your season. Allow God to redeem all the betrayal you've endured. God did *not* cause your betrayal. God did not send that person to you to do what they did to you. Listen carefully. God did not *cause it*, but He will *use it* to prepare you for what He has prepared for you. Please catch that. In other words, God wants to redeem it and use it.

Joseph's brothers betrayed him and threw him in a pit, and from the pit he was sold into slavery, and from slavery he went into the prison. From the prison he went into the palace. While in the palace, his brothers show up one day. He says this to them in Genesis 50:20 (paraphrased): "You meant it for evil against me to destroy my life. You meant to break me. You meant to wipe away my dreams. You meant to embarrass me. You wanted to annihilate and eliminate me. That's what you meant it for."

The Bible says, when Joseph was in the pit, his brothers remembered the anguish as he cried out, "Please don't leave me. Please don't leave me in this pit." But they forsook him in that pit despite his cries. *We left him in that pit.* They ignored his cries for help. They gloated over him. They meant it for evil, but God meant it for good, in order to save many people's lives.

I love the story of the couple from our church who've been clean and sober for over 30 years. They came out of a crazy lifestyle of addiction. Because of what's happening in their lives today, you'd almost think it was God's plan. They're leading thousands of people into recovery, impacting thousands of people through their ministry. God is using their lives and using their story.

The husband, Alan, spent time in prison. Last year he was recognized by the Washington State Governor as one of the state's Volunteers of the Year for his thirteen years of faithfully ministering to inmates in prisons. You'd almost think it was God's will for them to live crazy like they did so they would have a powerful ministry today, but it was not His will. However, He has an incredible ability to take broken places and redeem them; making a new tattoo. Make it a new story. Make it something we can be proud of.

In 2 Corinthians 5:17, Paul says, "So then, if anyone is in Christ, he is a new creation." *When* do I become a new creation? In Christ. In Christ I become a new creation. What is old passes away. LOOK! What is new has come.

If you are in a car, do you go where the car is going? The answer is yes. The other day my wife and I were getting in the car, and I told Miss Kelly to put her seat belt on. Better safe than sorry, because, "I'd hate to be driving down the road and have to hit the brakes and have you fly through the windshield and then run over you and have to live with regret the rest of my life. Put your seat belt on." I told you my mind is always planning ahead! The whole scenario played out in my mind. "So, put your seat belt on." The only way you don't go the way the car is going is unless you leave the car through the windshield. If you're in the car, you go where the car goes.

If you're in the pit, you go where the pit goes. If you are in Christ, you go where Christ takes you. *Look!* If you're in the car, you see the horizon and you go where the driver goes. If you're in the pit, you see the despair of life. If you're in Christ, you see blessings He has in store for you. He rescues you. He forgives. He restores. He redeems. Allow God to turn your betrayals into redemption and change the story of your life. Ask for His help to take off the old branding and put on the new.

Ephesians Chapter 4 says it this way: "Put off, concerning your former conduct, the old man which was corrupt according to his deceitful lusts, and be renewed in the spirit of your mind." Now, we *put on* the new man which was created according to God in righteousness and true holiness. Take off the old, put on the new. How? By renewing the spirit of your mind; renewing your thought life.

The stuff I'm teaching you in this book, I've worked on myself, my whole life. I still work on it daily.

As a young person, I felt so awkward, inadequate, and inferior. I knew I couldn't be the person God wanted me to be. As I matured, I used to go to really fancy hotels, but not to stay there. I was too poor to afford being there. But, I would go in because I felt intimidated to be there. I'd just walk through the lobby. You know, after a while something really interesting happened. I'd walk up to the door, and they would open it for me like I belonged there. They would greet me like I belonged there. *Wait, I'm just an imposter.* They treated me like I belonged there anyway. *Why are they treating me well?*

I started to recognize something was wrong with my thoughts. My thoughts kept me out of places I belong. My thoughts were keeping me out of places where people treat me like I belong there.

God, help me to take off the old. Renew the spirit of my mind, so I may put on the new. I live a blessed life. My life is so blessed, and I don't deserve it. But, I know how to receive it. I'm not going to project my rejection on God; my insecurity on God. If I do, I'm going to recognize it and take it off. I didn't earn my salvation – none of us earns salvation. We're not good enough for His salvation. I just have to take off the old and accept His new.

To escape the pit of betrayal, forgive those who betray you. Jesus is hanging on the cross and He says, "Father, forgive them for they know not what they do." That's powerful. If you want to get free, you're going to have to forgive. Not because they deserve it, but because *you* do. Not forgiving keeps you tethered to that past offense. Forgiveness is letting it go. Forgiveness is a decision followed by a process that leads to your deliverance. It's not an emotional thing. It's not a magical thing. *It's simply a choice.*

Offender, every time the memory of you comes to torment my mind, I'm deciding you're not going to occupy my mind anymore. I'm letting you go. I forgive you. I'm going to think about something else now. Do that as often as you need to do it, until that offender and their wound can no longer torment you. Continue saying out loud and in your thoughts, "I'm going to release you, I'm going

47

to release you." But every time you nurse it and rehearse it, and you fantasize all the ways you want to get vengeance—all the things you want to do to them to get them back—you fuel it and you feel it again. You can stop feeling it! Release them; let it go and come into a new season.

It's not over when God is in it!

WORRY WART

Nightmare tattoos are not the ones on your physical body, but the tattoos on your soul. Tattoos that happen in our hearts leave a mark on us that can stunt our growth. Tattooed hearts find it difficult to be grateful. Do you ever find yourself saying, "I would be more thankful if I didn't have so much pain in my life?" But, life is full of painful moments.

Certain things that happen really sabotage us. If we're not careful, the negative circumstances can swallow up our life, and become the theme of our life. The beauty of being grateful is what makes those difficult and awkward moments more bearable and more manageable.

The Bible says in 2 Timothy 1:7, "For God has not given us a spirit of fear." What robs us of our ability to be grateful? When a threat comes into our life. Threats bring fear. What the Bible is saying here is there is a mark of fear that tends to shape us. It's not from God, because God wants us to be shaped by His Spirit of love, power, and a sound mind.

One of the tattoo nightmares we're going to have to

overcome is the tattoo of major crisis and threats. Have you ever had a major crisis in your life? If you haven't, you just haven't lived long enough yet. Sooner or later everybody will deal with a crisis or a threat.

Here's the thing about a threat. Remember that God has not tattooed you with fear. It's not the mark that God wants you to be identified by. A threat is something that has just enough truth in it to be believable. When it has a bit of truth in it, our imaginations can start going off. Let's put it this way: a threat is something fear-based that starts isolating you. It puts you on an emotional island where you're all by yourself. You get out there on this island and your imagination starts running wild. The size of the threat, whether it's real or perceived, is going to determine the emotional intensity that ramps up in your life.

Let's back up for a second. How many times have you prayed for God to change your circumstances—that came as the result of a threat or a crisis—only to find out that God didn't change the circumstances? He just needed to change *you* and calm you down. For instance, you may give the car keys to a teenager, and they're two minutes late past their curfew. Instead of being home at 11:00, it's 11:02. You have enough truth for the tattoo of a threat. To put you on an island, to get your mind going. You're creating a whole world of *where are they at? What happened? What's wrong?* Can you relate?

Or, your spouse is deployed. They don't make their appointed phone call or Skype in at the appointed time. *What's wrong? Where are they at? Oh, God.* Panic sets in.

When threats happens, you feel it in your stomach. There's enough of the truth—they didn't do what they were supposed to do—to initiate worst-case scenarios flying through your mind. All of a sudden there's this feeling, this emotion, the heart rate starts picking up, and you start flushing. You've got these imaginations that start running out scenarios. *What could be happening? Maybe it's this or that...*

Maybe you and your spouse are in a tough season in your marriage and it's been kind of crunchy between you. He calls and says, I'm going to be working late tonight. You go, "Really? Are you trying to get away from me? Are you seeing somebody else?" God says, "I'm not going to put that kind of tattoo on you." That threat puts you on an emotional island that brings torment into your life. Your imagination gets going. God says to you, "I did not give you a spirit of fear, but of love, power, and of a sound mind."

Let's look at what the Bible says in Philippians 4 in the Message Bible. I love this: "Don't fret or worry." Let's pause right there. How many know when a threat or panic comes, you think, *what do you mean don't fret or worry? That's what I do! I've been practicing my whole life. I'm pretty good it by now, God. I've got this down.* If they paid people for worry, I'd be a wealthy person.

You should study out the word *worry* sometime. The Bible tells us don't worry. Don't worry. Don't worry. God admonishes us about worry. What happens when you start worrying? Your mind starts going in all different directions. It literally starts being divided into parts. Have you ever seen a person full of worry be able to make a major decision well? Did you ever see a person full of worry step out in confidence? *I'm worried if this is the right person. Should I marry him, should I not marry him? I'm worried if this is the right job. Should I take it? Should I not take it? I'm worried should I buy this or not buy this?*

Worry will divide you up into pieces. Have you ever heard the phrase, they're falling apart? Crisis came. Threat came. They're falling apart. That's what worry does. Worry is about falling apart.

This is why being thankful is so important. Let's be honest, it's easy to be thankful when life is good. What I'm trying to tell you is that life is full of pain. Being thankful is going to help you manage the worry and painful times. It's going to get you off of the island of emotional torment, because God has not given you that spirit. It's going to shift you from vain imaginations that run wild and create torment in your life.

Remember, you went down a whole scenario of why your teen was two minutes late. They show up at 11:05, and, "Mom, Dad, I'm sorry. I had to stop and get gas." But in that five minutes, you lived a whole eternity in hell. Your soldier finally gets through, and, "Yeah, I got held up." Suddenly you're relaxed. But for that moment between, you played out all kinds of crisis scenarios in your mind; worst-case scenarios. You go down certain pathways of worry.

Here's what the Bible says in Philippians, "Don't worry.

Instead of worrying, pray." Let petitions and praise shape your worries into prayers. Letting God know your concerns. Most people, when they are on the emotional island of fear, pray long and hard out of fear and not out of faith. They think it's their hard, long prayers motivated by fear that's going to get an answer.

God wants to know your concerns. In fact, let Him *have* your concerns. Cast them on Him and then get into His presence. Become tattooed by the Spirit of love, power, and a sound mind. Let God know your concerns, and before you know it, you'll sense God's wholeness, everything coming together for good, and will come and settle you down.

Honestly, God doesn't need to change my circumstances. Most of the time, He just needs to change me. If God changed me, I'd have a whole lot less stress in my life. I'd have a whole lot less fear in my life. I'd have a whole lot less worry in my life. Why? Because most of the threats that I have are only perceived, not real. If I perceive it as real and big, the intensity of that fear is going to be huge in me. God is saying, "Pull yourself together. You'd better get away from that worry, or you're going to fall apart." He's trying to get His peace to settle on you; in you.

It's wonderful what happens when Christ displaces worry at the center of your life!

FEARFUL IMAGINATIONS

Most people don't understand they've been tattooed by fear. When the fear and the crisis comes, it's always going to be bigger than it really is, because Christ is not the center of our hearts.

When He is the center, it's wonderful! It's amazing! It's awesome what happens when Christ covers over the tattoo. God can 'make over' the tattoo of fear, worry, and insecurity. It's amazing what happens when we move from being ruled by fear, to being moved by the love of God.

The Bible says in Proverbs 17:22, "A cheerful heart is good medicine." I need a lot of medicine. I can get negative in certain situations, and start worrying about this and fretting about that. You may need more medicine, too. A crushed spirit dries your bones. You just need to get singing; get praising. Start thinking about something good. Why? It's good medicine!

Your child was five minutes late. When we don't handle crisis well, or handle threats well, or handle those moments that are painful well, we often suffer more than is necessary. Maybe more conversation, more direction, or more discipline is what you need, but more fear is not. You don't need to be full of fear and go through torment.

God, change me in this moment. God, help me take my medicine right now. Help me to get my heart happy.

During the holiday season, most people are stressed out, burned out, and say things they wish they hadn't. When families get together for Thanksgiving, stressed-out people get hurt feelings. The week of Thanksgiving becomes a week when very little thanks was given. For some people, it's just about getting a couple of days off from work. For some it's just about eating turkey with family.

For you and me, however, thanksgiving should be a lifestyle. I hope you catch this. If you want to have a strong life, if you want to have a prospering life, if you want to have an overcoming life, if you want to have a succeeding life, you have to learn how to replace sin and worry at the center of your heart with Jesus Christ. We do that through gratefulness; through gratitude.

When a tattoo of crisis or threat comes, immediately get your mind moving in the right direction at its inception. Acts 16 is a story about Paul and Silas. They felt led by God to go to this particular city. When they got there, the people became angry at them. Paul and Silas were dragged before a judge. The judge had their clothes ripped off of them, ordered them beaten with many stripes, and thrown into the inner prison. If you felt like God asked you to do something, and this is what happens you, might you be a least a bit confused? Sometimes stepping out in God's obedience doesn't mean that everything is smooth. Stepping out in obedience is making sure that Christ is at the center of your heart. That you have the Spirit of love, power, and a sound mind.

When they were in prison, at midnight, they began to pray and sing songs to the Lord. Sometimes we read too quickly through these types of biblical stories. This is an important key to understand: when they begin to sing songs, there was an earthquake and the prison doors opened. So often, we think if we'll just praise the Lord, the prison doors will burst open. I really don't believe Paul and Silas were singing and worshiping God *to get* the prison doors open. They just loved Him.

Try to enter the story here, try for a moment. They were beaten severely. I think when they threw them into the inner prison, they didn't have any rights. I don't think the accommodations were comfortable. I think it was dirty, nasty, and painful. I think they had open wounds on their bodies. The reason it is midnight and they're awake is because they are in so much pain they cannot sleep.

In this moment they choose to be effective people. They choose to be healthy by choosing to worship God. They're not complaining about their beating. They're not complaining about the jail. They're just worshiping. In that moment they are trying to manage the pain they're in. Gratefulness is a tool to help us stay strong in life. Gratefulness, worship, and being thankful are tools to help us endure the challenges of life. Most people are waiting for life to get good to become thankful. I'm telling you, when you become thankful, life will get good.

Listen to this scripture out of 2 Corinthians chapter 10. Verses 3-5 says, "Though we walk in the flesh [meaning this natural body], we do not war according to the flesh." You and I are in a battle. Our battle, as Christians, is not with people. "For the weapons of our warfare are not carnal." They're not of this world. "But are mighty in God to the pulling down of strongholds." You have weapons. Do you know what they are? Do you know how to use them?

Have you ever been to somebody's garage and they're really good at working with wood? They've got all kinds of wood-crafting tools. Have you ever noticed that people who have some skills usually also have lots of tools? You're in their garage and you're looking around. "Man you've got a lot...why do you have so many hammers? Why do you have so many different chisels? Why do you need so many different kinds of saws?"

You go to somebody else's garage and maybe they're a mechanic. They have wrenches and other various tools. You think, *man they've got more tools than they know what to do with.* But they probably know how to use every single one of them.

Next, you go into Miss Kelly's kitchen. This is a true story. We are putting up cabinets in our garage for the rest of her extensive kitchen supplies! Our garage is not for my stuff, no. Our garage is for *her* cooking stuff. We are more equipped than any restaurant I've ever seen. We play games with her, challenging her to see if there's any cooking tool in the world that we might think up, only to find out, "I've got that! I've got that!" She even has a blow-torch for crème brulee. She's has everything! Of course I don't have permission to use *any* of them, but I do appreciate her skill set. What are you saying, Pastor?

Realize that you, too, have tools. You have weapons. And one of those weapons is gratefulness. When you use your tool of gratefulness, you express *Christ is the center of my life, not fear. Christ*, not worry. *Christ*, not crisis. *Christ*, not intimidation.

I will not live on the island of emotional torment. I will empower myself. I will become an effective person, because I will use the tools that have been given to me. Just because you walk into somebody's garage and they have a heap of tools, doesn't mean you know how to use them. You might walk into Miss Kelly's kitchen, but it doesn't mean you would know how to use all her tools, either.

Tools are used by skilled craftsmen. If you want to lead a skilled life, you need to know the weapons of your warfare and learn how to use them. One weapon is gratefulness. It is a powerful, powerful weapon.

Listen to what the rest of 2 Corinthians 10 says about *casting down arguments*. Strongholds are belief systems that get us blocked in. Arguments and imaginations get going in your mind. Every high thing that lifts itself up against the knowledge of God must be cast down. "Bringing every thought into captivity to the obedience of Christ" means I've got to be responsible to capture my thoughts, stop arguing with myself and make those thoughts come into alignment to the obedience of Christ.

USE YOUR WEAPON

I really want you to be equipped when it comes to using your weapon of gratefulness. Let's break this down:

Being thankful changes—or refocuses—our perception and redirects how we see things in our life. Matthew chapter 6 discusses our spiritual eye's perception. If your eye—your vision—is healthy, your *whole* life will be full of light.

Everybody has a vision, a perspective, a perception. But, if your vision (your spiritual eyes) are unhealthy, your whole body will be full of darkness. If the light within you is darkness...most people don't think their perception of life is distorted. Most people don't think their perception of life is dark. Most people justify their perception of how they see life as being correct. The older you get the stronger the perception that *this is the way I see life, and I see it right!* But God is saying that if the light you see is darkness, how great is that darkness.

Think of it like this: you have a perspective, and you have a vision. Happy people, successful people have strong, positive focuses in life. If you took your life and it was a canvas; a ten foot painting that covered the story of your life, many different colors and shapes would be on it. The canvas is beautiful, but there was this one place in your life where your marriage out of order. A two-inch square of something dark shows up.

We can easily miss the whole focus and decide to focus on that two-inch square that's out of order. Maybe it's a damaged spot. Maybe it's an unfinished place. Instead of standing back and looking at the whole canvas, we just narrow in and start looking at that two-inch square until it fills up our whole perspective. You may have a certain negative perspective about your relationships, about your marriage, about your job, about your career. If so, your whole focus is on this two-inch problem.

The Bible says that if you shift focus to see what is good instead, your whole life will be full of light. If you'll understand and start looking for what is good in life, start declaring and counting your blessings...it's like taking your medicine. Seriously, life is going to be full of challenges, but purposefully set your attitude

If I were to go to your house, you might have 500 channels available on your TV, but your TV is probably set on four or five favorites. Your vision is set on something. Tomorrow a morning alarm clock will go off. It is already pre-programmed and set, and all you have to do is turn it on. It's set! It's set to move you from unconscious to conscious. You may not like that moment of transition, but it's time to get out of this state and into this state.

Being thankful is something you have to set your mind on. I *will be* a thankful person in the midst of whatever is going on, good or bad. I'm not going to let my gratitude be predicated by what goes on around me. I'm going to let my thankfulness be predicated by Christ being the center of my life.

In your home, you have a thermostat and you set the temperature to anything you'd like. You set the climate in your house. Your attitude should be like a thermostat, not a thermometer. Some of you only reflect the temperature in your life. But God wants you to *set* the climate of your life by paying attention to the power of focus. I am choosing to take my medicine and be grateful, so that I do not live with a crushed spirit and a crushed heart. I will not allow fears and threats near me.

I'm not saying fear won't ever get going. But the moment you recognize it, say, "God, I'm not going to let this thing win. I'm going to take my focus off of this crisis, and I'm going to start being grateful." The truth is that often your attitude is more important than the facts of your circumstance. It's more powerful than your opposition. It's more versatile and creative than your circumstance.

You show me someone with the right attitude, yet with opposition against them, facts against them, circumstances against them, and I'm going to show you someone who is a person worth watching. They are the classic David and Goliath; this is the classic underdog situation. This is a person worth watching, because somehow this person is going to end up on top.

The Bible tells us in 1 Thessalonians 5:18 to give thanks in all circumstances. Not *for* all circumstances or *for* everything, but *in* all things. You don't thank God for something evil. You don't thank God for somebody betraying you. You don't thank God for wounds. When that wound happens, it's powerful to still give God thanks and praise in your circumstance. Why? Give thanks in every circumstance, because this is God's will for you in Christ Jesus.

People often say, "Well, I don't know what God's will is." I do. It's right there: GIVE THANKS IN EVERYTHING. *No, I want to know what I'm supposed to do.* No...just give thanks. Why is this important? Remember, we talked about not worrying? Often, God can't give us direction until we get in another frame of mind. A lot of us are trying to get direction through worry. God says, when you get in another frame of mind, then I'll give you directions.

This is brilliant! You could get directions if you got out of worry. You could get directions if you got out of fear. You'd get directions if you got out of the nervousness of that situation. Now, I'm not down-playing tough situations, saying those things aren't real. Problems come. I am saying to manage it, overcome it, get through it, survive it, defeat it, because God has not given you a spirit of fear, but of love, power, and a sound mind.

Positive people are grateful, thankful, and worshipful. Those attitudes are so powerful. People like that live bigger lives than bad attitudes. People with grateful attitudes, love bigger, love deeper, and make bigger commitments. Have you ever seen someone with a bad attitude make big commitments? Mentally file this away and watch for this to happen in life.

You ask people with bad attitudes, and they'll say, "I make big commitments all the time." "Well, what's your big commitment?" "I have to go to this job and I hate it. I work where the people are so mean to me. This woman I'm married to, she's just so draining on me." "Ummm...dude, that's not a big commitment. This is just daily living! You're stressing through each day without good reason. You aren't even able to dream because your mind is struggling with simple, daily stuff."

"So, what's difficult about the job?" "They expect me to be on time." Really?

Please listen to me – if the light within you is darkness, how great is that darkness. Start picking up the tool of grace. God's grace gives us things we don't deserve. Ask Him to redesign bad attitude tattoos into gratefulness.

I know I don't deserve any of the good things in my life, but I know how to receive them. I am a receiver of God's goodness. Christ is the center of my life. I work hard, I live big. But I understand I need to stay grateful, or get on an island of torment, emotional and mental, and get tattooed by the enemy or circumstances in life, versus being tattooed by the goodness of my God.

10

REDIRECT YOUR THINKING

Being thankful redirects our thoughts. Have you ever noticed when you're trying to get your thought life under control, and you say, *I'm not going to think that*, and then you think that? Have you ever noticed when you want to think about something, and all of a sudden, you find yourself daydreaming, and you're down the road with something else?

Our minds have the ability to be very undisciplined. They like to do whatever they want to. It's like having 'monkey-mind': thoughts swing around in your head and jump branch to branch. Maybe that next branch is called *fear*. When the monkey lands on that branch, it starts looking around and gets all kinds of imagination creativity in that moment.

Then, it decides to jump again and it comes to a new branch. This branch might be called *lack*. You start seeing all the financial problems in your life; all the bills you have and worries about retirement. After you get tired of that and the monkey decides it's time to jump to another branch, it finds *worry*. Then it starts meditating on the kids and what's going on.

You have lots of things going on in your world, and your mind jumps from situation to situation and starts going negative. You're saying, *be positive, be positive.* But, you keep finding yourself daydreaming about the negative.

I'm about to give you gold. Catch this and it will help you.

The focal point of your thought life is tied to your mouth.

When you start talking, your mind starts focusing. You may not realize this fact. God doesn't want us to pray because it's an empty exercise. He knows that when we become grateful, it starts focusing our mind; aiming our mind on a target.

The Bible says that our tongue is so powerful, life and death are in the power of it. Those who love it—life or death—will eat its fruit. Matthew 12 says, "A good man, out of the good treasure of his heart, brings forth good things." How am I going to bring forth good things? By declaring them out of my mouth. "An evil man, out of the evil treasure of his heart brings forth evil things." By your words you will be justified, and by your words you will be condemned.

In James it talks about maturity. True maturity is the ability to master what you say. How many marriages have been destroyed because someone didn't master their tongues? How much grief is in a home because parents said something to their children or the children said something to the parents that created lasting wounds?

Words are powerful, for life and for death. The Bible says it's so powerful that it's like a little rudder that can steer a massive ship. A bridle in a horse's mouth has the power to redirect a powerful, mighty animal. It's like a little fire, one match igniting an entire forest ablaze. It's like a few drops of potion poured in a well, poisoning everyone who would drink from it. Life and death are in the power of this little 'member' of our body.

When you and I begin to be grateful, gratefulness redirects our minds. Being thankful refocuses my mind and redirects my thoughts when I'm in a crisis. That's why a cheerful heart is good, like medicine. When you're in a crisis, start looking back at God's past goodness and start declaring it for the present.

God, I've got this storm coming up in my life, or I've got this thing I'm afraid of. I'm just going to suspend it for right now. It's barking for my attention. I'm just going to set it aside. What I'm going to do right now God, I'm going to recall your goodness in my life. I'm going to remember the time that you were there for me. I'm going to remember the bill you helped me pay. I'm going to remember the door you opened for me. I'm going to look back over the goodness of my life.

Do you journal about answered prayers? I encourage you to do this, so in a crisis you can take an inventory of your past and how God has been there for you. Take inventory of all the assets in your life that are precious to you.

Years ago, I met a gentleman named Peter Daniels. He got born-again at a Billy Graham Crusade. He was a fifth-generation welfare recipient in Australia, and grew up in poverty. As a teen, he was kicked out of school. He had no education. He was a brick-layer. Once he became born-again, he started reading scripture and learning how God wanted him to be successful.

Now Peter is one of the most successful men in Australia with thousands of people working for him. There was a point in his life where he had a choice to buy food or buy something for his spirit. He bought something for his spirit. In one of the dire seasons in his life, he had a business crisis and needed to get a loan from a bank. He went in and started talking to the banker. The banker said, "Daniels, your situation is so bad, you don't have enough assets to cover this loan. What we're going to do is deny your loan." Peter looked over the table at him and said, "Sir, you've not considered *all* my assets." "What do you mean?" "I don't think you've considered my wife. And I don't think you've considered my children." He started listing lots of other relationships and life assets. The banker began to weep, because he had riches the banker did not have, and approved his loan.

So often, we get tunnel vision about where we're at. We just need to stand up and say, "You know what, fear? I know you want me to get on that island of imagination, but I'll get back to you in a moment. I'm going to spend some time over here, pulling through the journals of my heart, pulling through the journals of my life, about how God was there for me, and what God did for me. I'm going to start declaring with my tongue, with my mouth, God, thank you for Your faithfulness. God, thank you for Your goodness." This will change our focus. Decide to change your focus with your tongue to get into a different position, and a different thought.

Being thankful redirects my thoughts. Thankfulness releases God's presence in my life. Now, God is always with us. The scripture says He never leaves us nor forsakes us. Even so, sometimes there are times like, *God, I know You never leave me, but where are You?*

When you begin to be grateful and thankful, it releases a thing called the *felt* presence of God. When that *felt* presence of God comes, His peace is released. You immediately move from stressed out to peaceful. Nothing has changed except you. You go from *what's going on?!* to, *I've got hope! Everything's going to be all right!*

You literally go through an emotional transformation. Intense emotions, intense thoughts, and intense feelings are all gone. Instead, there's a strength, a peace, and a confidence. In a moment, *you've* changed.

In Isaiah chapter 61, God wants to impact His people, and "to console those who mourn in Zion," which would be His people, His family, "to give them beauty for ashes and the oil of joy for mourning." Notice how God wants to change the tattoo. Do you see that God is trying to give you a tool here? He wants to give you joy, beauty, and the garment of praise for the spirit of heaviness.

The New English Bible says it this way: "A mantle of praise in the place of discouragement." The Contemporary Version says it this way: "Joyful praise to replace a broken heart." The New Century Version says, "Clothes of praise to replace the spirit of sadness." The New International Version, says, "A garment of praise, instead of a spirit of despair." God is trying to clothe you, trying to turn your ashes into beauty. *I'm trying to turn your mourning into joy. I'm trying to change your despair, your discouragement, your brokenness, by putting on garments of praise.*

What I'm saying to you is this: we don't praise because we're supposed to; we praise because it's the lifestyle of overcomers. We praise because it's a tool to manage disappointments, threats and crisis in our life. A garment of praise is what makes us the head and not the tail, the top and not the bottom. We're being influenced and shaped *not* by the circumstances around us, but by the circumstance within us. Worry has been replaced by Christ being King.

God is not afraid. He's not intimidated. He does not have lack. That's why He says, "When you've been tattooed by Me, it's with love, power, and a sound mind."

God wants His church to be a house of prayer. "Be high and lifted up in my world, Lord, be lifted high. Devil, I don't care what you try to tattoo me with, you can tattoo me with a threat, but watch how I respond to you. I'll do what I've got to do, I'll manage what I have to manage, but in my thought life, I will not be tormented by you. I'm going to be a grateful, powerful, thankful person. God's going to get me in peace and I will get through."

11

THE INK IS DEEP

In Genesis 2:25, the man and his wife were both naked and they felt no shame. When God created the earth God, He did not create shame. In fact, in the Bible He specifically said, *I did not create shame. I created Man, I created Woman. They were free, they were forgiven, and they were beautiful.* They had nothing attached to them in the form of shame.

Looking a bit further into Genesis 3:6-13, it's the story of Satan coming to deceive Eve. I love the section where it says, in verse 13, "the Lord God said to the woman, 'What is this that you have done?' The woman said, 'The serpent deceived me and I ate.'" How many times in life has the enemy deceived you by telling you and stamping you with something and you consumed it? How many times has he said, *you are this, or you are that?* And you said, *you're right, you're right.* You ate it, you consumed it. It's no longer a free life. The ink, the stamping on some of us is deep.

Many times we are justified in our pain. Some of you have been victims of physical abuse, verbal abuse or sexual abuse. I, in no way, want to belittle or minimize what you have been through, but, here's what I want to say: the enemy wants you to consume it so much and tattoo you so deep that you'll never live a free life. The opposite is God, Who wants you to be completely released from guilt and shame in your life. He wants your testimony to change the world.

The definition of guilt is *a feeling of responsibility or remorse for some offense, crime, wrong, etc., whether real or imagined.* You can have real things happen to you and feel guilty. You can have imaginary things happen to you and feel guilty.

And how about shame? Shame is *a painful feeling arising from the consciousness or the awareness of something dishonorable, improper, or ridiculous done by oneself or another.* There is a difference between true guilt and false guilt. I had a big revelation recently. I always thought guilt and shame were really bad things. I started studying guilt. I realized that guilt sometimes comes in the form of a little conviction from the Holy Spirit. I realized that sometimes there is that momentary feeling of guilt that makes you lift your head and go, *whoa, whoa, whoa, whoa. Wait a minute. I'm one shift away. God, I've got it, I got it. I'm one shift away from making a breakthrough.*

That is true guilt, which comes from the conviction of the Holy Spirit. Sometimes you're working or doing household tasks and God will make you aware of a misstep in a split second. But, understand, that guilt, too, if it's never dealt with, will eventually turn its way into shame. We are famous as human beings for making our feelings the reality.

Don't get stuck in emotions. Recently, someone was talking about how their brain is so busy. My brain is extremely busy. I completely identify with him. I might walk by you, and I might be so busy in my brain that I don't really see you. I have much love for you, but I might not see you. So, sometimes we can get stuck in those moments, and stuck in the emotions of it all because we had a feeling. We had a feeling of rejection. We had a feeling of fear. We had a feeling of sadness. We had a *feeling* that led us down the road in our heads that wasn't real. We had a feeling that grew into this massive mountain, when really it was only a little pebble.

So, what do we need to do in order to get our feelings under control? We need to gain understanding. Visit Proverbs 3:13. I love to read Proverbs. It says, "Blessed is the man who finds wisdom, and the man who gains understanding. For she is more profitable than silver, and her gain than fine gold."

When we internalize our abuse, when we internalize our feelings and our behavior, it attacks our identity. When it all goes inside, we start to stir and manifest this thing that isn't real. All of a sudden, our identity says, *they rejected me*. All of a sudden, we internalize it. It says, *I am worthy of being rejected. I was abused. I am worthy of being abused.* All of a sudden we have this identity that lives on us. We might as well have a tattoo stamped on our forehead or arm, *I Am Worthy of Being Rejected.* That momentary guilt, that moment can turn us from guilt into shame.

Did you know that shame is the root of almost all compulsive disorders? Compulsive disorders usually start out with a feeling; a strong emotion that compels you go and do something to make yourself feel better in the moment. Compulsive disorders are things like drug addictions, eating disorders, sexual promiscuity, gambling, etc. Those bondages grow out of *one single thought*. That dangerous thought can eventually turn your entire identity around, in the negative, unless you capture it early. It is a horrific, vicious circle that happens when the enemy starts to talk to you.

Here's what happens: we feel guilty, then we have shame. We accept shame. We consume it. We eat it. Then, we go and do something compulsive that we regret, heaping more guilt on, and we get back into more shame. The cycle continues on…we go and do something else that makes us feel guilty. We get back into guilt and then back into shame. A compulsive disorder—being in bondage to sin—goes around and around. The ink of your tattoo goes deeper, and deeper, and deeper.

Guilt and shame cause us to walk around heavy. You carry the weight of this thing that's been placed on you by the world; by the enemy. Sin creates shame, if not properly dealt with. We are all sinners. The world has damaged a lot of us. However, even if we are victims of abuse, we do *not* have to live a victim's life. Change starts with the Holy Spirit.

Here's a key to peace. If you live your life in worship, you probably lead a pretty clean life with a light heart.

But, we all have a sinful nature, so, again, even as you read this, some of you are thinking *oh yes, I'm a sinner. I grew up in a church where they told me I was a sinner. I had no value...just junk.* That is the enemy trying to hold you captive. You have the choice to let it go, and step into His presence. Accept freely His forgiveness. Or, you also have the choice to live with the ink going deeper, and deeper, and deeper.

Forgiveness...I like to call it freedom. Freedom is the opposite of shame. Freedom is forgiveness. Have you ever been in an argument with someone, or had issues with someone, and your emotions are bound up with the whole mess? Then, all of a sudden, you have a freeing conversation where you know you're forgiven? As you walk away, your heart feels light, free. Forgiveness is freedom. Shame is a stronghold that is keeps you bound. We somehow get into the mindset where we are told we are worthy of abuse, and we end up agreeing with it. It matches with our identity.

I challenge you, instead of sticking with the mindset of, *I am worthy of abuse, therefore I am worthy of nothing good,* I want you to get the mindset of, *I am worthy of forgiveness, therefore I have it all.* We've got to shift our minds. Guilt is recognizing that you have done something wrong. We've all done things wrong. We're all guilty. *Got it. I messed up. Great. I'm going to let myself move on and try not to do that again.*

12

GUILT AND SHAME

Shame is the intense feeling that *who we are* is wrong. Guilt is seeing what you have done. Shame is seeing yourself as a failure. God will convict our spirits to get us to adjust our life. Guilt is looking at the sin. Shame is looking at yourself attached to that sin.

God separates our sin from who we are. God doesn't see us for our behavior. If you're a parent, you get this concept. Children are not born with shame. The day a child is born, they do not care what you think. They scream and cry and tell you exactly what they wanted. They live under no condemnation; under no shame. We are not born with shame. God does not see us as our sin. He sees us as His children.

We might have kids who are struggling with stuff. When kids are small, they have different kinds of struggles than older children. But, you see them going through stuff at every age. You see them living with the shame and the guilt, and you still love them. You still want to forgive them, no matter how much they have screwed things up in their life, even if they've rejected you. Through their battles, you still want to love them. That is how our Father sees us. He does not attach us to our sin.

I want to caution you, though – we, at some point, discover that guilt and shame can work for us. I'm going to be a little tough here, but I want to challenge you. Often, when we put guilt and shame on other people, it gets us the results we want. Oftentimes, if we put guilt and shame on other people, it will control them to behave how we want. All of a sudden, we put a heavy weight on them. That heavy weight may get them to adjust things, but to fulfill *our* flesh.

Pastor Trisha Ferguson, our worship pastor, tells this story: I have two daughters: one is six years old and the other is three months. Getting out the door to anywhere is a struggle. One day I was trying to make breakfast, my spouse was in the shower, and my infant is crying. So, I put her in the swing. It's a season of managing chaos. I hear when they're teenagers they sleep a lot, so I'm looking forward to that day. But, we realized recently that with the age gap in our kids, we're going to have teenagers for about 15 years!

Anyway, I glance over at my beautiful, sweet, funky six-year-old who was over at the baby swing visiting her sister. That swing was rockin' and rollin'. She had turned the swing up to level 6 — max power — which is ultimately meant for larger babies. I see the swing going like gang-busters, and I see my daughter delighting in this! I exclaimed, "Whoa, what are you doing?!"

All of a sudden, I felt the shift. I walked over, turned it

down and said, "We don't do that and here's why..." But, here's what I could have done very easily and out of my flesh, said, "Hey, what are you, an idiot? Shame on you! Knock that off you jerk!" We, as parents, oftentimes, just make mistakes. I've made plenty of mistakes as a parent and have had to come back and say, "You know what, honey, I didn't handle that right." At age four, five and six, they're still cool with that. But make those small adjustments quickly.

Never say to your children, *shame on you*. It might get you the results you want for the moment, but in the long term, you are placing guilt and shame on your child, because you are part of their identity. Even as I say that, I can hear you thinking, *oh no, I'm screwing up my kids!* Please hear this: we make mistakes. We move on. We ask for forgiveness. We love, we love, we love, and we love. We restore, we restore, we restore, we restore.

13

THE VOICE IN OUR HEAD LIES

The voice in your head is a liar. I hate to tell you that, but it's true. Be conscious of your self-talk. If your thoughts are stuck, your emotions will be stuck. A lot of times we don't have control over our emotions. But we do have control over our thoughts.

In Hebrews 10:19-25 there is a call to persevere. It says, "Therefore, brothers and sisters, since we have confidence to enter the most holy place by the blood of Jesus, by a new and living way opened for us by the curtain, that is, His body. And since we have a great Priest over the house of God, let us draw near to God with a sincere heart and with the full assurance that faith brings. Having our hearts sprinkled to cleanse us from a guilty conscience."

God wants to cleanse us from a guilty conscience. We can feel shame and condemnation, and, oftentimes, it gratifies our flesh in the sin nature. But, it's not of God. As we learned in Genesis, God did not create guilt and shame. The Word also says that if it's not of God, we *can* take control over it because Christ Jesus is in us. You are one thought away from freedom. You are one word, one declaration, and one moment away from freedom.

Does your mind tell you what you are not? Or does your mind tell you what you are? Do we have a righteous conscience or a failure conscience? When those thoughts come to us, we have to learn how to grab hold of them. We have to learn to recognize what kind of voice we're hearing. We have to get to the point where we say, *gosh, I feel super heavy. Why am I feeling down?* Once we grab hold of the root, we can take control of it with our words. Your words, words of affirmation are so powerful.

Vision boards are popular now, which is a godly principle. God wants you to see who you are even when you are not there yet. Does that make sense? What your thoughts focus on will change you and will shift you one way or the other. We have the authority to change shame into victory.

What are the weapons we fight with? Gratitude, taking our thoughts captive, forgiveness, and a new one: we fight with our words. Where do we get the right words? In the Living Word, the Bible. In the Word, God tells us how much He loves us, that we are champions, how we overcome through Him, tells us we are worthy of the sacrifice of His Son. He says we are the head and not the tail, and He wants to position us above all things in the world.

That's amazing truth. While reading that, if you said, *that's not me*, you need to grab a hold of that thought and shout the enemy down. The weapons we fight with—our words—demolish strongholds.

II Corinthians 10:4-8 says that the weapons we fight with are not the weapons of the world. Praise God! Because the world is a little rummy. The world is a little messed up. I need something *beyond* what the world has to offer, because the world messes with me sometimes.

It's so simple, but speaking God's Word has the power to demolish strongholds. Strongholds are those things that keep you heavy and hold you captive. We demolish arguments and every pretension that sets itself up against the knowledge of God. We take captive. To take captive means we take the lie, put it in a place where we don't see it, we don't hear it, we don't feel it, and we don't allow it to exist. We isolate the lie and move it out of our lives. If it pops up again, we've got to punish every act of its disobedience.

"If anyone is confident that they belong to Christ, they should consider that we belong as much to Christ as they do. Even if I boast somewhat about the authority the Lord has given me for building you up, rather than tearing you down, I will not be ashamed of it." Paul said that to the people of Corinth (2 Cor. 10). Some of you even feel guilty in boasting in the authority that God has given to you. I encourage you to read 2 Corinthians 10. It says, whatever God has given you, you boast on it. If God has given you authority to battle things, and you take authority and you speak it out of your mouth, do it, because the Word says you should.

God is an amazing God!

Prayerfully start to recognize and prayerfully identify the words in your head that are not of God. Start to recognize when you feel unqualified for something. *You are not qualified; you have to do this XYZ before you are qualified.* If you spend your whole life feeling unqualified, you will never get to be place of being qualified.

I want you to prayerfully consider the things that you say to yourself; the voices in your head that lie. I want you to write down a truth and put it someplace you will see it every day. Maybe it's stuck to your bathroom mirror, maybe it's posted on your refrigerator, maybe it's on your steering wheel, or maybe it sits on your desk at work. Wherever it is, stare repeatedly at the truth.

Take those wrong mindsets and lies in your head to the Word. Read Proverbs, Psalms, and Hebrews, and all the other amazing books in the Bible that will tell you who you really are and about your great worth. If you're struggling with being worthy, write down with a big black marker: *I Am God's Child Worthy of Everything.* Write it down. Maybe somebody told you one day that you weren't pretty. Post *I'm the Most Gorgeous Thing God Has Ever Created on This Earth* right onto your mirror. Boast on the authority that God has given you.

Maybe someone said that you're not very smart. Maybe you spent your whole childhood believing that you were dumb because someone said you were. You write *My Intelligence Was Created by the Same Man Who Created the Entire Earth and the Entire Solar System...He Created My Mind for Such a Time as This*. Read those truths every day and take hold of your worth. Kill the lies and nurture the truth!

14

HEALING LIGHT

Let the Light in. In studying about tattoos, I learned a lot about the tattoo removal process. The most successful tattoo removal is laser removal. That is so amazing! As I was reading and researching through it, essentially, the process of tattoo removal is putting light on the old tattoo itself. It changes the pigment of the skin over the ink. It works the same for heart tattoos.

When you continue to put God's light, through His Word, through worship, through fellowship with other people who speak light and life into your life, you will see a process happening: the stamp and the ink, even though it's deep, will rise up and out. You've got to take that laser, that Jesus laser and dig deep.

Here's another fact: how large or how deep the ink goes determines how long the removal process will take. Look at the symbolism here. You can't have really deep ink—deep shame—and overcome it without going through the removal process of getting underneath the light of God. When you get underneath His light, He will start to plow away. He will start to heal your heart. All of a sudden, all of the justification you had for the abuse in your childhood, or the abuse of your relationships, or the abuse of whatever it might be, fades. Something changes, and it's like, *I'm good. I'm good.*

My heart goes out to those people who must be living under the same shame they tried to pass on to me. Grace, mercy and light covers the stamp that they have stamped you with. Get under His greatness. He cannot reveal Himself more to you without you seeking Him out. Our God is a God of relationships. He's not going to invade you until He's invited. God did not invade my heart until I invited Him to be a part of it. He is waiting for you.

I love the Bible story of the woman with the issue of blood in Luke 8:43-48. Verse 47 says, "The woman." There was this woman who had been shamed by the world. She was shamed by the world based on physical circumstances. Does that make sense? No one told her a lie or harmed her; it was based on circumstances. She had a medical issue that the culture shamed and rejected her for, with no fault of her own. She was moved aside, and treated like a leper. She was unclean.

This woman knew what people were thinking, just like some of us believe that message of *we don't want to be in your presence. We don't want you around us. We don't want you to come to church. You're not accepted.* This woman heard all of those things.

She reached out for His robe anyway and managed to grasp the bottom hem. She was seeking Him out. Even in her seeking, she was invaded by His power. "Then the woman, seeing that she could not go unnoticed..." She still wanted to be hidden. She realized in that moment that she couldn't go on unnoticed. Jesus wanted to hear from her. She came trembling and fell at His feet. In the presence of all the people she told why she had touched Him and how she had instantly been healed. And He said, "Daughter, your faith has made you whole. Go in peace."

When you seek Him out, those moments are peaceful. When you seek Him and you put the light on your situation, there is peace. Shame and false guilt are based on deception. They are not of God. You have been lied to; deceived into believing that you should be ashamed and are not worthy. When the light comes, those dark lies must flee.

Romans 8:1-2 says there is no condemnation for those who belong to Jesus. Through Jesus, the laws of the Spirit of life have set us free from the law of sin and death; the law of shame and death. How long have we spent trying to recover what we already had all along? How long have we spent trying to recover from shame, to seek forgiveness, to seek peace, and to seek refuge, when, ultimately, we've had it all along? You just had to lift your head, get into His presence, and let the light in.

God makes all things new. Your Father does not want you live a heavy, bogged-down life. He wants you to have the freedom of His presence, the freedom of His peace, grace and mercy to live in you all of your days.

He wants the peace that surpasses all understanding to dwell in you and come out of you.

Here is the key about His light:

Instead of being depressed about mistakes, get excited about forgiveness.

Set your mind on forgiveness and the accepting of that forgiveness freely, instead of setting your mind on mistakes. We all make mistakes. We all have made big mistakes that we need forgiveness for. We are fleshly human beings who are doing our best to get out of our junk and into dwelling in His presence.

Go out in the world and take His presence with you. That's right – you take His presence with you wherever you go. How? By speaking His Word, through prayer, and by worshipping.

I listen to worship music in the car. Sometimes, I've got to stir up the Holy Spirit in my heart. We've got to get the truth inside us, so we can get excited about forgiveness. That way, your mistakes no longer identify you. Rather, forgiveness identifies you.

Jesus' grace and mercy changes who you are as a human being. You can get His grace and mercy so saturated on yourself that it flows out to other people. That is what will attract the world. What are we called here to do? Preach His gospel. It's not just me and other pastors, though. *You,* too, are called here to preach His gospel; to *be* His gospel. We've got to figure out how to let Him make all things new inside us.

Because of Jesus' work on the cross, we are called and able to live a shameless life. Get excited about releasing the shame off of your life! Get excited when you make a mistake and see yourself get up, dust off, and start again. Recognize when you've just made a mistake, ask forgiveness, and move on.

There is good news: what the enemy has placed on us in the form of shame, will be God's greatest glory. What am I talking about? The greater your story about being an overcomer, the greater His glory is shared. There are people all over this planet who need to see someone who has gone from their situation to being an overcomer. They need hope! You need hope! There are some of us who can fill an entire week of programming on Jerry Springer's show. It is okay! Because you know what? You can come out on the other side with victory.

God is calling you to take your greatest weight and failure and allow Him to shine His light on it. He says, "Children, I want to release you from it, so you can live that testimony out and it can be for my glory! Not for your glory, although you get to enjoy the benefits of freedom." Hallelujah! So your greatest overcoming can be His greatest glory.

15

THE FREEDOM IN AN APOLOGY

One day, I put this question up on Twitter:
How would you feel if someone who wronged you sincerely apologized to you? How would you feel if someone who hurt you, disappointed you, betrayed you, or did something wrong to you actually said, "I'm sorry?"

Here are some of the responses:

"I would feel thankful."
Let me get this right: somebody wronged you, they apologized, and you feel thankful? Just think about that – that's powerful.

"I would feel humbled. Grateful. Blessed."
It's an interesting thought, isn't it? *You wronged me, you apologized, and I feel blessed*. If that's true, I need to start apologizing more, and bless more people.

You might be more familiar with this:
"I would feel shocked! In awe! Stunned! Overwhelmed!"

Here is another interesting one I received:
"I would feel set free."

I would feel set free – wow. As believers we are constantly working on our part of forgiving people. Let's be honest. There are people that let us down. There are people who have disappointed us. There are people who have wounded us, betrayed us, or violated us. We're trying to do the Christian thing and forgive them and let them go. But if we were honest, we are struggling with it. If we were honest, they keep coming to our mind. We're so ready to be done with this. So ready to be beyond this. So ready to be down the road. But, the reality is that *I'm still wrestling with it. I wish I could get over it. I feel stuck at times.*

Just think how helpful it would be if the person you're trying to forgive simply said, "I am sorry. I was wrong." It's like, *Hallelujah! You just set me free! I am so blessed, I am in shock right now that you would even say something like that.* That apology has the power to heal the wound on our soul.

Some of you are trying to do the right thing. You're trying to get over a hurt. You're trying to forgive that person. But, you're still struggling with it. All because of a lack of an apology. I believe God will help you with that. Someday you might hear the words, "I'm sorry, I was wrong. Can you forgive me?" But, you may not. You may never hear those words. You're intimately acquainted with the struggle of overcoming an offense and trying to do the right thing, when you lack an apology.

Here's something I want you to think about. Is there somebody on the other side of your behavior, of your words, who is struggling to go forward in life because they're waiting for an apology from *you*? While that person may not come and unlock us, maybe we could unlock somebody else. In the process of unlocking somebody else's tattoo, we also cleanse ourselves of a life of regret. We unload those regrets. Let's be honest, it's so much easier to forgive when an apology and repentance is manifested.

In fact, I'm going to help some of you right now. The Bible tells us to forgive, even as Christ has forgiven us. Guess what you need for the forgiveness of Christ to impact your life? You need repentance. Without repentance, the full impact of His forgiveness cannot impact your life. When we offer Him repentance, we experience the full impact of His forgiveness. So, you're no different than Christ. There's people who need to hear an apology. You need an apology because it causes you to struggle without it. There are others who struggle without your apology.

I was watching a documentary that was really powerful. I didn't get to see the whole thing; only about thirty minutes. The name of it was really strange; it was called "The Redemption of General Buck Naked." While the title was funny, the documentary was not.

It was about a general in Africa in the nation of Rwanda. I don't know if the title 'general' was appropriate, but 'terrorist' would be. He would literally come into these villages with nothing on, with his band of raiders, and commit incredible atrocities; murdering, pillaging, terrorizing, and violating. The documentary was about his journey. Somewhere along the way he had become "born-again," and then had actually become an evangelist.

He was traveling to visit the same cities where he had previously raided and left damage in his wake. In the story, they were interviewing him, and then they would cut away and talk to some of the people who had been victimized by him. You hear him describing his journey and how he was on a new road of redemption, but you also hear other journeys from the people he once terrorized. They described how horrible the memory of this person was and what he had done to them, destroying their lives. Then, they'd be informed that he's preaching about Jesus now. They were cynical. *But he's full of the devil. How can anybody even think to be as evil and cruel as this man?*

The documentary team set up meetings for him to meet with people he had violated. When he met with these people, he would say, "Tell me your story. What did I do to you?" That's powerful right there. One woman shared, "You came to our city, and I started running with my daughter. You grabbed us and you hit my daughter who was just a little baby. You hit her with a rifle. She's damaged in the eyes now. She's seventeen years old. You went into my house and you killed my husband." He says, "I'm sorry. I'm not the same person. Can you find it in your heart to forgive me?"

You can see the buildup: this person is so full of anger,

frustration and hurt. When the General asked for forgiveness, her tears began to flow. He made it easier for her to move past her nightmare; her terror. It was also interesting that the woman's daughter—who could not have remembered this, who lived with the mark of his brutality—she's crying too, knowing that this person has taken responsibility for what he had done.

Then it went on to a second story; the story of a young man who may have been in his late teens or early twenties. "You came to my town and you killed my family," he said. "I have no one." This angry young man repeated, "You took everything from me, I have no one." The General looked at him and said, "I'm sorry. Can you forgive me?" This young man began to cry, broke down in huge sobs and said, "I forgive you." And this repentant terrorist said to him, "I know I can't make it right, but if you'll let me, I'll be family for you." He embraced him again and accepted his offer.

An apology can heal deep wounds. How often do we leave people suffering? How long have you and I been suffering for the lack of an apology? How long do we leave others suffering for the lack of an apology? How many teenagers grow up in anger, and rebellion, and defiance, all because of a lack in a parent not saying, "I'm sorry – I was wrong – will you forgive me?" How many wives are withdrawn and have declared an emotional war, all because a harsh husband would not say, "I was wrong, and I ask you to forgive me." There's a false balance that exists without the justice of an apology.

I understand that an apology alone does not solve everything. But, in our marriages, our families, and our relationships, let our heart's cry be more for reconciliation and restoration than for justice. That's a powerful phrase if you can understand it.

Our hearts cry more for reconciliation and restoration than for justice.

Now, justice *is* a good thing. But justice will not satisfy what you really want in your most personal and intimate relationships.

In Matthew chapter 9: 2-13, Jesus said, "Those who are well have no need of a physician." He's not talking about physical sickness, but those who are sick in their soul, in their heart, in their mind, in their spirit. *But, go and learn what I'm talking about. Go and learn what I'm saying. I desire mercy, not sacrifice.*

"I did not come to call the righteous, but sinners to repentance." He came to call sinners to repent. Is there anybody that is not a sinner saved by grace? So, guess what you and I need to be good at? *Repentance.* We're going to mess up a lot. Isn't it interesting, we mess up a lot, yet apologize little? Jesus is saying lack of repentance makes your heart sick.

Notice that God is a just God; He demands justice. The One that is speaking in those verses is the One we will stand before and give an account of our lives to. The God of justice is saying that He has satisfied the need for justice through Jesus' death on the cross. But what

He wants from us is an apology. I'll pay the price, you just give me an apology.

Sometimes a simple *I am sorry* can satisfy a deep wound. This is an extreme example, but what if you have a family member that is murdered, and the person who murdered him went to jail for the rest of their life. Justice has been served: a life for a life. But, would your soul really be satisfied? What is your deepest want? You want what was taken away, you want the person you loved back. So, justice itself doesn't satisfy what your heart really craves, which is reconciliation.

Think of it like this: if an employee steals something from a company and he's caught, he may be taken to court and convicted and end up going to jail. Justice is served. Chances are he won't ever work for that company again, right? Let's say he steals something, and then becomes repentant. He goes to the owner and says, "You know, I have really messed up. I have betrayed your trust. I've betrayed your confidence in me. I have done this, and here are the steps I've taken to make this right. I want you to know I don't ever plan on doing this again. I'm taking responsibility for my actions. Can you find it in your heart to forgive me?" That person could potentially stay on with the company because he's taking responsibility and offering an apology.

16

Apology Invites Mercy

In the book of Genesis there's an incredibly beautiful story. I want to illustrate it, and then give you some practical steps on how to give an apology. Our hearts cry for connection. Our hearts truly desire intimacy, not justice. That's what Jesus is saying: "I desire mercy, not justice; not sacrifice." He is a just God, and justice must be served. That's why Jesus went to the cross and died. He took care of the justice part. You and I can't pay for the damage we do. Very few of us are in a position to pay for the damage we create.

The power of an apology invites mercy.

Mercy can release and satisfy the wound that's been tattooed there. Some of you are struggling to get past the issue of forgiveness because somebody hasn't paid that one little thing: an apology. *I am sorry*. Everyone has a sense of morality about what's right and what's wrong. When something that's right with you is wronged, you feel violated. In a relationship, when you feel violated, you feel unloved. In the absence of an apology, a young person can grow up unloved by their parent. In the absence of an apology, a person can go years feeling unloved by their spouse.

The Bible tells us to repent. We can practice repenting; work at repenting, but chances are most of us feel like repenting is out of our comfort zone. We're more comfortable being offensive than we are at repenting. When we're wounded, we don't feel loved by that person. We want justice. We want that wrong to be made right. *Make it right!* The offending person may never make it right for you. What can happen is, we want a sense of justice. That sense of justice, if it's delayed, will cause us to do one of two things: get vengeance or condemn ourselves.

We may take steps into our own hands: vengeance. And *vengeance is mine*, you say. *I will make you pay. I will exact a pound of flesh.* All of a sudden we become vengeful. We don't see it that way, though. In our perspective we're just giving them what they deserve.

If they're going to be cold to me, I'm going to be cold back to them. If they're going to be mean to me, I'm going to be mean back to them. They hurt me, I'm going to hurt them back. Now, we don't see the path we're on; the path to becoming an offensive person ourselves. Therefore, we don't see our need to repent, because *the only reason I'm mean, ugly, crooked is because you made me this way. It's your fault I'm this way.*

We don't see ourselves clearly while we're in the process of taking justice. That's why the Lord says, *justice is Mine. I'll settle the debt. You just practice mercy, forgiveness, and repentance. You just do that, and we're good. I'll take care of the vengeance. You're not qualified. You get all emotionally heated up. You're not qualified to be judge.*

But, if we don't seek vengeance, we go the other way; we condemn ourselves. If justice doesn't come, then *maybe I deserved this. Maybe if I'd have been a better person, maybe they wouldn't have abused me. If I'd have been a better child, they wouldn't have hit me like they did. If I'd have been a better person, my husband wouldn't have left me. Somehow, this is the way people like me should be treated. Because in the absence of justice, somehow I deserve this.*

We either take matters into our own hands or *we* are the guilty person (even though we're the victim). Some of you do that with God all the time. You're trying to be so good. You're trying to pray so much. You're trying to get it all together. You're trying to have a level scorecard with God to make Him love you. Scripture says that "while we were yet sinners, Christ died for us." He already loves you, even in your mess.

We say, "All I want is an apology. Is that so hard?" And trust me, it *is* hard. God said He'll pay all the debts. *You cause all the damage; I'll pay all the debt. I just want one thing: for us to have a relationship. An apology. Repentance. If you can't repent, I'll pay all the debt, but we can't have a relationship.*

That's why He can pay the price for people to be saved, but some still go to hell. He paid all the debt, but they choose to go to hell because they don't want to own up to their piece; to their transgression. Their response to God's provision is silence. All God wants to hear is, "I was wrong. Yes, I did it. You paid it, but I did it. Thank you. Thank you. Thank you. I feel blessed, I'm so blessed by You, God."

Joseph's father was Jacob, who was one of the patriarchs of faith. He's one of the pillars of God, but his family was dysfunctional. You cannot believe how messed up this family was. It gives all of us hope. If you read the Bible, you may think, my family has problems, but nothing like these families in the Bible!

Let's talk about Joseph again. Joseph has a bunch of older brothers, but they come from different mamas. Joseph's mom had one other son named Benjamin. Jacob loved Joseph's mom more than the other moms, so Joseph and Benjamin are special. That's a problem right there...every time you've got more than one woman in the house, that's a problem. It's never going to be a good idea. So, strife abounds in their home, because Joseph's gets special treatment, creating jealousy and envy in all the other children.

Joseph, at seventeen years of age, shared a dream with his older brothers that they didn't like. They see him coming one day and say, "Here comes the dreamer. Let's kill him." Judah said, "No, let's not kill him – there's no money in that. Let's sell him as a slave and get some money out of him. We'll tell Dad a beast ate him and we'll go party on the money we made out of selling Joseph into slavery." Joseph ends up in Egypt as a slave. Seventeen years old, no education, no resources, no support system, no family. Paraded in the slave market, stripped naked in a foreign land, he's sold into slavery.

This is incredible victimization. But, as a slave he kept his head and refuses to get offended. He begins to do well as a slave. Then the slave-owner's wife accuses him of committing adultery, which he did not do. Another violation. Now, the slave owner says, "Whoa, you tried to mess with my wife? Prison for you." Now he's in prison. He keeps his heart right. Overnight he's got favor with the jailer, because he has the ability to interpret dreams and tells Pharaoh, the king of the land, the interpretation of his dream. Pharaoh makes him second in command...of an entire country. Overnight he goes from rags to riches and becomes the second most powerful man in all the land.

There's a regional famine coming. That's what Pharaoh's dream was about. There's going to be a famine, and Joseph knew what to do about it. He stored up food in the seven good years so during the bad years they'd have food. The famine comes, and all the surrounding nations have no food. Everyone starts coming to Egypt to buy food, and Joseph helps make this nation incredibly wealthy and powerful!

Joseph's brothers travel from way up north in Israel—because they are starving—to get food. They arrive and meet this person in charge of food distribution. Joseph recognizes his brothers, but his brothers don't recognize him. He accuses them of being spies and locks them up for three days. He spoke harshly to them. Oh, can you imagine the power! What would you do with that much power to wield?

Being accused of being a spy is a death sentence. He could give the charge against them and have each and every one of them executed. Nothing could stop him;

nothing but his own conscience and spirit. Joseph's wrestling this thing through. He's speaking rough to them. He's asking, "Where did you come from and who are you? Are there any more of you?" They accidentally let out, "There's our father, and we left one younger brother." "What's his name?" They say, "Benjamin."

Joseph says, "Here's the deal. I'm going to let you go. But you've got to bring your other brother back here to let me know you're not lying. And, Simeon, you're staying here to ensure they come back."

Simeon, the Bible says, was a cruel dude. Joseph thinks, *I'm not letting you guys know who I am, because if you know, then you're going to kill my brother. And the cruelest one of you I'm going to keep right here, because I don't trust you.* Simeon was so cruel that when his father Jacob pronounced blessing, he said to Simeon, "I have no blessing for you. You're going to be absorbed into the tribe of Israel." That's why there's no tribe of Simeon. He was so cruel that his blessing was removed. Joseph decides to leave him there in prison. He was a dangerous man. Remember, Joseph had the power to kill them all.

Joseph gives them some food for the journey and to take home to their father. The other brothers head home. They forget all about Simeon. They leave him down there in jail. Interesting thought: we don't grieve very long over mean people. We don't grieve over people who fight to be right, but we do grieve over people who care for us.

They finally go back when they're running out of food. Jacob, their father, says, "I need you to get some more food." They said, "Look Dad, we cannot go back without Benjamin." Jacob says, "What? There's no way! He's my special boy. I don't like the rest of you. I could care less about Simeon. You're not going to ransom Benjamin. I've already lost Joseph, the child of my special wife, and I'm not going to lose the second child by her." Yeah! It's messed up! It's in the Bible. This family is messed up!

They starve for a little while longer. They're pressuring him, and he's refusing. "Okay, we're all going to starve, so you might as well take my son, Benjamin." Judah says, "Dad, I'll bring him back. I promise I'll bring him back." So they travel again to Egypt; this time with Benjamin.

In Genesis 43 it says, "Joseph lifted his eyes and saw his brother Benjamin, his mother's son, and said, 'Is this your younger brother of whom you spoke to me?'" At this point, it's probably twenty years later. "'He said, God be gracious unto you, my son.' Now Joseph's heart yearned for his brother." Remember he craved reconciliation. "Joseph made haste, and sought somewhere to weep. He went into his chambers and he wept there. He washed his face and came out and restrained himself and said, 'Serve the bread.'"

Watch this: he sees the brother he has craved connection with all these years. He has all these other brothers, they're family, but they have rejected him. He doesn't reveal himself to them. He has the power to

103

destroy them but he fears God. He restrains himself. He's working through this thing called forgiveness. But there's still no apology.

When he wants connection, he says *I will not show vulnerability in front of you.* He runs into the other room...cries like a baby...washes himself off...puts himself together and comes back out with this dignified posture again and serves the food. I hope you catch this. In the absence of an apology, people don't show their vulnerability in the same room with them. They run to another room. *I'll be vulnerable in another room, but I won't do it in front of you, because you're not a safe person to me.*

I'm talking about our marriages. I'm talking about our families. I'm talking about in churches. I'm talking about in the relationships that should matter the most. We won't become vulnerable to a relationship we crave a connection with in the absence of an apology.

The servants set Joseph at a place by himself, and the brothers by themselves. The Egyptians sit by themselves because the Egyptians could eat no food with Hebrews, for it was an abomination to the Egyptians. So, catch this picture. The Hebrew people have to sit at a table, and the Egyptians have to sit at another table. Because to the Egyptians, the Hebrew people are an abomination!

Joseph, who is not an Egyptian, sits at another table. His brothers, who are an abomination to him, have to sit at another table. You've got these separate tables going on. Does that describe somebody's Thanks-giving holiday? When somebody walks in one room, somebody else walks out. You get into the same house, but you avoid being in the same room. You know exactly what I'm talking about. They walk in...you walk out. The family dynamics are there. A cluster of people migrate to one table and talk about the abomination at the other table.

He doesn't reveal himself, yet. He feeds them and sends them back home with all kinds of food. He lets Simeon go. But, he still has a plan. He says to his servant, "Take my cup and put it in Benjamin's bag." Joseph sets up the brothers. "I talked about it at dinner. The cup that I love, put it in Benjamin's bag."

They start riding off on their way home. They got Simeon back. They got some food. Everything's good. Great...they're out of there. *That was a close one. We're outta here! Wait...here comes the Egyptian army.*

Run them down! There's a thief among you.
What?
Someone has stolen the master's cup. His favorite cup. His special cup. The cup that no one should touch. One of you took the cup.
We didn't take the cup, we promise! We're not like that.
No, one of you took the cup, and the guilty will pay.

Sure enough, they soldiers start going through everyone's bags. No cup here. No cup yet. They finally go into Benjamin's bag. Lo and behold, the cup! It is in Benjamin's bag because Joseph had it put there. The brothers are all freaking out. The soldier says, "Don't worry about it, the only one of you who has to go into captivity is Benjamin. The rest of you can go home. You didn't steal anything. He stole something, so he must go back."

What is he doing? He's saying *the only one I can have a relationship with, the only one I can share a table with, the only one I can reveal myself to is Benjamin. The rest of you are hardhearted, mean-spirited, and don't like me. I have the power to kill every one of you, and I chose not to. I'm not going to seek justice. But I'm not going to seek a relationship with you, either. Because there's no apology. Benjamin didn't harm me. Bring him back to me and the two-of-us will live a better life.*

Some of you are in that struggle. *You* live a better life, but you're struggling. You don't want to bring others on the journey with you, because they won't apologize. Even though you want to bring them on the journey, you don't feel that you can trust them. You won't harm them. You can only do good deeds for them, but you can't have a relationship with them. *I'll do you something good. I'll buy you gifts, I'll do something nice for you. But, no, there's no relationship here. There's no mercy here.*

What happens next? Judah steps in. Remember, Judah is the guy who said, "Don't kill him. Let's sell him and make him a slave." Judah gets all of his brothers to follow Benjamin back to Egypt. Judah begins to intercede and plead for his brother Benjamin. Here's his prayer, found in Genesis 44: "Your servant became surety for the lad for my father's sake. If I do not bring him back from you, then I shall bear the blame before my father forever. Please let your servant remain. Let your servant, me, Judah, remain, instead of the lad, as a slave to my lord." Whew! Did you catch that?

Let me be a slave to the man I sold into slavery. He doesn't even know what he's saying, or who he's saying it to. *Let me be a slave to the man I sold into slavery.* How healing do you think that might've been for Joseph to hear? How powerful was this moment? "For how shall I go to my father if the lad is not with me? For I see the evil that would come upon my father." There's a healing that's going on here. Could he be expressing a touch of regret and responsibility for the past?

Now the next chapter, says it this way: "Then Joseph could not restrain himself from all those that stood before him. He cried out, 'Make everyone go out from me!' So all the servants left the room while Joseph made himself known to his brothers." Verse 14, says, "Then he fell on his brother Benjamin's neck and wept, and Benjamin wept on his neck. Moreover, he kissed all his brothers and wept over them. After that, his brothers talked with him." Are you catching this? The breakthrough came after he heard a heartfelt apology.

*I messed up at another point in my life. I'm not the same person I used to be. I can't do this again to Dad. I wouldn't hurt Benjamin like I hurt...him...*Judah's not saying Joseph, but Joseph is reading between the lines. Joseph breaks down. He's no longer running to weep in another room. He's weeping in front of them. Our hearts crave reconciliation and restoration more than they crave justice. He had many opportunities to get his justice. What he really wanted was reconciliation.

17

FIVE-FINGER APOLOGY

What does a sincere apology look like? Many of us have never had it modeled to us. What is usually modeled to us is outbursts and harsh words. Mom and dad are in control. Brothers and sisters are out of control. But, we don't see the apologies. Maybe apologies happen in private, but what do they look like?

Isn't it interesting that when it comes to public displays of negativity, we try to clean it up, privately. How cool would it be if dad sat his children around and said, "You know, I spoke really harshly to your mom the other night. That's not the kind of husband and father I want to be. I'm sorry for that. It's wrong to do that, and I just want you to know I'll never talk to her that way again. I'm sorry."

Now, he may have apologized in the bedroom, but the kids didn't see it. Some of you haven't seen the spirit of apologies, the spirit of repentance, so we're left to try and figure it out.

Here's some help: simply remember the 5-finger system.

Finger #1: I Am Sorry.

Those words are like magic. Those words are so powerful! So therapeutic! So healing! "I Am Sorry. Sorry." Sorry for what? Get specific. "I don't know why I'm sorry. I'm sorry that you're sorry! I'm sorry that you're mad! I'm sorry that you're crazy! I'm sorry that you're sad! I'm sorry that you're crying! I'm sorry that you're sorry! Because if you weren't sorry, then I wouldn't be sorry!" No...this is not what I'm talking about, at all.

"I'm sorry that I told you I would be on time, and I was late, and you made dinner and it frustrated you. I'm sorry because I spent more money than our budget allows. I'm sorry because I said some mean things to you and that must have made you feel really small, hurt and put down." Be specific and never, when you're saying I'm sorry, never put a "but" in it. The minute you put a "but" (an excuse) in, the apology vaporizes.

Saying the magic words, "I'm sorry for yelling at you," works well. However, if you add a *but*... "But, you made me so mad! I'm sorry for committing adultery. But, if you were just more sexual. I'm sorry for spending more money than was in our budget. But, if you would just give me more." Do you see that you've canceled everything you just said?

Here's another thing people do. They apologize, and then they want the other person to apologize, too. "I said I'm sorry, where's yours?" No. You just leave it alone. We're not talking about them. We're talking about you. When you say *I'm sorry* to Jesus, don't expect Him to say I'm sorry, too. Say, "I'm sorry I wasn't there for you. I'm sorry I didn't love you more. Sorry I didn't listen more."

Finger #2: I was wrong.
"I was wrong for what I said. I was wrong for what I did. I was wrong for the way I behaved. I was wrong." See, sometimes people can say, "I'm sorry that I hurt you, but, I'm not wrong." Please catch this. Some people can say *I'm sorry*, but the other person still doesn't think they've taken responsibility. When you say you were wrong, you're saying you take responsibility. Here's the problem with that. Some people don't want to accept responsibility because they think it's a sign of immaturity. But listen carefully. Healthy people, effective people, have the capacity to say I was wrong, and therefore are able to make changes.

Finger #3: I will do my best to change.
This is the heart of real repentance. "I'm going to think differently. I'm not going to keep doing that same thing. I know I've been struggling with this addiction. I'm going to change. We may have to make a plan. We may have to write something down. I'm going to start going to Celebrate Recovery. Or, I'm going to start going to church. You can hold me accountable. I'm going to change. Here's my plan. I'm changing. I don't want to be that person anymore."

Communicating the intent to change and the desire to change, plus the plan to change, is most effective. That genuineness creates a lot of grace. You'd be surprised how much grace will cover. You can fail your way into success if you're at least going in the right direction.

Finger #4: What can I do to make it right?
How do I make restitution? How do I pay for the damages? Sometimes, in a marriage, that may mean opening up some time on your calendar. My wife and I went on a special trip last year. We got out our calendars and said, "Okay, let's make some time together this year." The previous year got way too busy for us, and I felt neglectful of our relationship. We made time, and I'm making restitution. I'm paying in time, making up for a season of wrongs with a season of rights.

Maybe it's words or maybe it's just sitting down to listen: there are all kinds of ways to make restitution. Maybe a gift could be given. Find a way to make restitution when appropriate.

Finger #5: Can you find it in your heart to forgive me?
You can go through, "I'm sorry. I was wrong. What can I do to make this right with you?" But, it still doesn't indicate that you want a good relationship in the future. There's something positive about, "Can you find it in your heart to forgive me?" It says, *I want a relationship with you.*

A spouse could say, "I was wrong for this affair. I'm sorry that I'm having this affair. I'll do everything I can to make the divorce equitable to you." That's not an apology: that's an exit strategy. When you say, "Can you find it in your heart to forgive me?" you're saying *I want a relationship.*

Sometimes we're afraid to say that, because after we've gone through this whole act of humility, "I'm sorry....I was wrong....I want to change...What can I do to make it right?" saying, "Can you find it in your heart to forgive me" gives them power back. It's like saying, *I humble myself to you.* Something powerful happens when they say, "I forgive you." Healing gets released.

This is the forgiveness and repentance process as Christ commands. Repentance and forgiveness. Forgiveness and repentance. That's a powerful combination.

18

BLIND SPOTS

Have you ever embarrassed yourself? Take a moment to remember that instance. Would you ever share the story of it?

I was talking to my wife the other day, and I asked her, "Did you ever have anything embarrassing happen to you?" She said, "Yes." And I asked, "Do you want to tell me?" She said, "No." I said, "I won't tell the church or include it in the book." She responded, "No, I just don't want to tell you, period!"

That's hilarious, but isn't that the truth? We have embarrassing moments happen to us, then we wish we could forever forget them, bury them, and remove them from all consciousness. On the other hand, it's amazing to me how many people do embarrassing things and purposefully put it on Facebook, Twitter, and YouTube. It doesn't go away, people!

I'm going to talk about the nightmare tattoo of foolishness. We sometimes embarrass ourselves, and thankfully God wants to heal and cure us of these tattoo nightmares, also.

What an amazing Artist God is, and what amazing, transformational work He can do in our lives with the embarrassing things we've done. When it comes to physical tattoos, again, I hope you understand I'm not against tattoos. The whole idea of a tattoo nightmare is people going to pick out a design, paying to have it stamped on their bodies, and then becoming embarrassed by it. People pay for the tattoo, chose it, and actually sit through the pain of it. That's the way it goes, but we can still embarrass ourselves.

The scripture says in Proverbs chapter 3:35, "Wise living gets rewarded with honor." Wouldn't that be true? Like when we make good decisions, good things happen. *Wow, yes, I'm proud of myself!* We get rewarded for making good decisions. But read the rest of the verse. "But, stupid living gets the booby prize!" Have you ever gotten one of those? Have you ever gotten one of those recognitions for stupid living?

Proverbs 10:23 says, "A foolish person enjoys doing wrong." Wrong can be fun and fun can be daft. Eating a gallon of ice cream every day can be fun, but it will kill you. Smoking a pack of cigarettes might be fun, but it will kill you. There's a lot of fun stuff that just gets you the booby prize. A foolish person enjoys doing wrong. "But, a person with understanding enjoys doing what is wise." I love that it's not about whether it's right or not; just do what's wise.

Do you ever hear people say, "Well, I don't agree with that, I don't think it's right?" It doesn't matter if it's right or not – it's just wise. It's just the boundary between foolish and wise. Foolishness doesn't like to recognize authority. Foolishness thinks it's better than the authority.

Here's my true story:

I was teaching one weekend on being thankful in every situation and every circumstance. While driving to church, I was having fun driving faster than I should, because I thought the speed limit should be faster than the posted speed limit was. I thought it was humorous…I got pulled over for driving too fast on my way to church. Ironic…I'm on my way to church, I'm serving God, preaching about being happy in every circumstance of your life, and I get the ticket booby prize. The policeman wrote me one of those love letters for foolish living. Do you understand? I embarrassed myself!

It was classic. I'm just going to be happy right here in the middle of my foolishness. "Thank you, sir. Could you hurry, because I am in a hurry? Do what you've got to do quickly." I usually don't go more than a month without embarrassing myself.

Most of the time we embarrass ourselves because of our blind spots. Trust me, if I had known that police officer was there…it would have been different. He was not in a regular police car. Apparently, it really was a police car. It looked more like an SUV until his special, *pull over now* lights came on, and then I realized he was not a regular car. It was a blind spot. We usually embarrass ourselves because of blind spots. If we could see our blind spots, we wouldn't do dumb things, right?

I remember as a kid, I'd get dragged to church. It was either church or beating, so some days I took the beating. I'm just kidding! That's not true...but still, I had to go to church. If you've been in church as long as I have, you realize that people are creatures of habit. For example, you probably sit in the same or close to the same pew in church every week.

As a kid, I always sat in the back, so I could get out fast. And, when everyone closed their eyes to start the closing prayer, I'd sneak out. On Sunday, don't get any ideas please. There was this lady who always sat in the second row; second row, left side. Without fail, every week, she would get up in the middle of the pastor's message and go to the restroom. Without fail, every week. I was a kid and I was checking everyone out; who does what, who falls asleep, you know…

Now this was a heavier gal. She was slow in getting up, and she just kind of shuffled. I don't know if her feet ever went off the floor. Inevitably she would start working her way to the back, and we would watch her coming. This was every week. One particular week, she was unaware that after she went to the restroom her skirt did not make it past her pantyhose. The skirt was tucked *into* the pantyhose. It scarred me as a young child!

I started laughing – it was comical. As she made it slowly down toward the front where she always sat, all the people in each row she passed started quietly laughing. Their shoulders started bouncing up and down like a tidal wave moving through the church, from the back to the front. She sashayed slowly all the way down the middle aisle. The pastor was trying to figure out *what's going on* because of the tidal wave of laughter! This poor woman had a blind spot. Talk about how we embarrass ourselves because of blind spots.

Isn't it interesting that the place where we think we can see—with our eyes, or hear and perceive with our ears, or our taste, our smell, or any of our senses—can be our biggest blind spot? We have perception, but we really don't. We *think* we hear, but we really don't. We *think* we have a taste or a flavor, but we really don't. Our blind spot is in the place where we *think* we're the most perceptive. That's what leads to foolishness and pride. We think we know, but we don't know. We think we see, but we don't see. We think we hear, but we don't hear. It leads us to living in a blind spot.

This blind spot can embarrass us. The thing about a blind spot is that it can go from embarrassing to devastating. A blind spot can cause an accident. All kinds of things can happen to you in your blind spots. A blind spot is usually the result of two things: foolishness or pride.

Foolishness is just a lack of common sense, and is really the result of immaturity. The problem is that some people grow in age but don't grow in common sense. They don't learn that if you keep talking to people in that way, you keep ending up with broken relationships. Foolishness is a lack of understanding; a lack of comprehension and good judgment. We get into trouble when we're foolish. We didn't have the awareness to know we were walking down the aisle with our skirt tucked in behind our pantyhose.

The other part of this is pride. Pride is arrogance, defiance, being unteachable. It's resistance and self-justification. It's without restraint. The Bible says, God hates pride. He resists the proud. If I'm trying to get God's help, being proud is not the way to get it. Pride is a confidence; an elevated confidence.

To be clear, I believe in being confident. I believe in being reliant. I believe in being an effective person. But, it's also important for you to understand where that ends and where to have dependence upon God. When you try to be all things unto yourself without recognizing your need for God or His wisdom, that's where it becomes arrogance instead of healthy self-confidence. It's the result of foolish pride, and it can go from simply embarrassing ourselves to more devastating consequences.

In the book of Judges there's a story about a leader named Samson. He has a vow and covenant with God. God has given him supernatural strength. He's able to defeat Israel's enemies. He's been called by God for a purpose. But, he hooks up with woman named Delilah, whom he had no business being with. She makes a deal with his adversaries, the Philistines, that if she finds out where his strength comes from, they will give her a boatload of money. She's in!

She starts pressing Samson. She says, "Samson, where do you get your strength?" Now, remember, he loves this woman. He has a huge blind spot because this woman does not love him. She's using him. She says, "Samson, where do you get your strength?"

"Oh, if you don't tell anybody, and you take a brand new bow string, one that's never been used, and tie me up with it, I will become like other men, and be powerless." He falls asleep. She says, "Samson, Samson, wake up! The Philistines are coming!" And guess what? He's tied up with a bow string! That *should* be a clue! All of a sudden he jumps up and breaks the bow string and goes and defeats the Philistines. *Interesting. I told you what made me strong, I take a nap, and find myself in a bow string. Hmmm…*

Can anybody see this coming? Not Samson. *I got it. I can handle this woman. I'm strong. I'm powerful.*

She says, "Samson, you lied to me. Where do you get your strength from?" "Okay, I'll tell you. If you tie me up in a brand new rope, I'll be like other men." He goes to sleep. She ties him up. She says, "Samson, Samson. The Philistines are coming again!" And sure enough, he's got a rope on him. Interesting, again. He told her a rope, he's got himself in a rope. Can anybody see this coming, except Samson? He's got an enormous blind spot that's going to lead to devastating consequences. He breaks the ropes off and goes and defeats the Philistines.

"Come on, Samson, you told me you loved me." The

third time, she says, "Why don't you tell me the truth?" "Okay, I'll tell you! See these long beautiful locks? If you weave them into the loom of the weaving machine, then I would be powerless, and I'd be defeated." He wakes up and his hair is woven into the loom of the weaving machine. She says, "Samson, Samson. The Philistines are coming. They're coming again!" He shakes that weaving machine off his head and goes out and defeats the Philistines. Can anybody say blind spot? Man! This woman is not your friend! She is not! You do *not* have this under control!

Have you ever seen anyone struggle with alcohol? "I got it, I got it! It's not a problem." At what point would you call it a problem? "I've got my finances under control." At what point would you admit they are out of control? By the time you've lost your house and your car? At what point would you admit they're out of control?

In Judges Chapter 16, she says, "How can you say, I love you, when your heart is not with me? You have mocked me these three times. You have not told me where your great strength lies." Now, this woman does not love this guy. Everybody can see it but him! "It came to pass, when she pestered him with her words and pressed him so that his soul was vexed to death..."

If you pester a man every day, he'll eventually tell you anything you want to know. He'll just give up in life. She's pestering him every day of his life; badgering and battering. "Where's your strength? Where's your strength?" Notice, it vexed his soul. Most of the time we make foolish decisions because we choose poor relationships. We get talked into doing things we wished we never would have done. Why did we do them? Because somebody pestered us into it.

Let's be honest enough to say, "I found myself in an environment I wished I hadn't been in, because the people I hung out with encouraged me to go there." Some people have a tattoo that somebody else talked them into. But, they didn't want the tattoo. "Oh, you'd look good in that tattoo. That would be great on you!" They're talking you into something that they wouldn't do for themselves.

It's critical that you understand that most foolishness comes into our lives because of the relationships we choose to partner with in life. To understand this is wisdom. Some of you have relationships that really don't want you to attend church. They want to talk you out of it, and convince you to do something else with your life. May I say that those relationships are not good for your destiny? I'm *not* talking about breaking a marriage covenant, but Samson isn't married to Delilah. He needs to cut that relationship off...but he didn't.

Delilah vexed his soul and he told her all his heart. He tells about his covenant. "No razor has ever come upon my head, for I have been a Nazarene from my mother's womb. If I'm shaven, my strength will leave me, and I will become weak and become like any other man." Listen carefully. Samson had done something he should never have done. There is a part of you that you should never give to anybody, but God alone.

I love my wife, and I'm called by God to love her with all my heart. I love my children and I'm called by God to love them with all my heart. But there still must be a place that I reserve for God, and God alone. If I don't reserve a relationship with God, I won't know who I am with my wife. If I don't reserve a relationship with God, then I won't know who I am with my children. If I don't reserve a relationship with God, then I don't know who I am with you, my reader. There is a part of you that must be kept for you and God alone. Any relationship that would want to come after your destiny, or come after your relationship with God, or come after that part of you that belongs to you and God alone; those relationships will devastate your life.

Notice she pestered him, pestered him, pestered him, and finally, he gave away his heart to her. In essence, he said, *I know I can't trust you, but I'm bonded to you. So, I'm going to put my life on the line for you.* He made a foolish choice because of his blind spot. But, he's still thinking he can handle this relationship.

Remember the blind spot of pride? Pride is the strength of sin. God hates pride. He resists the proud. The reason that pride is the strength of sin is because it puts us beyond God's reach. As long as I'm in a state of pride, God can't reach me. Have you ever noticed that we usually have to become broken before God can reach us? Not that He wants us broken, it's just that pride produces brokenness in our lives. It's in our brokenness that we're humbled. Finally, then, we are ready to receive; to become teachable and not so defiant. As long as we're in pride, God hates it because He can't reach us.

How many marriages are destroyed because somebody didn't say, "Hey, you need to stop talking to your spouse that way…?" How many marriages are destroyed because a mentor didn't step in and say, "You know, you're too busy with your career and with other things, and you need to focus on *this* thing…?" And remember, because of pride, we don't receive wisdom, and so we lead ourselves into brokenness.

So, how does the story end?

"When Delilah saw that he had told her all his heart, she went and called the lords of the Philistines." Wow – she's doesn't waste any time. "'Come up at once for he has told me all his heart.' So the lords of the Philistines came up to her and brought her money in their hand. She lured Samson to sleep on her knees. Then she called for a man and had him shave off the seven locks of his head. She began to torment him." Isn't that amazing? She betrayed and taunted him.

I can almost hear her calling out, "Samson, the Philistines are upon you as before!" But his strength had left him! "'The Philistines are upon you!' He woke from his sleep and said, 'I will go out as before as other times and shake myself free.' But he did not know that the Lord had departed from him. The Philistines took him, gouged out his eyes, and brought him down to Gaza. They bound him with bronze fetters. He became a grinder in the prison. However, the hair of his head began to grow again after it had been shaven." Are you catching this story?

Samson's thinking, *I got it. I can handle it. I handled it once. I handled it twice. I handled it three times.* But he did not realize that he gave his heart away and he lost his strength, and the Spirit of God had departed from him. He found himself defeated. His blind spot had created devastation in his life. Notice his eyes were gouged out, but long before he lost his physical eyes, he'd lost his ability to perceive; he'd lost his ability to see what was happening. He lacked good judgment.

PRIDE

Can you say, *yes, there have been times, because of my lack of good judgment, I've really hurt myself, I've embarrassed myself, and gotten myself in trouble.* I don't think there is one person on the planet that can't say that. Everyone has been touched by a tattoo of foolishness and the tattoo of pride. The tattoos of foolishness and pride create all kinds of needless afflictions in our lives.

Habakkuk chapter 2:4 says, "Behold, the proud." Take notice of the proud. Observe the proud. Everyone has a perspective about how to approach life.

As a pastor, I am constantly dealing with people. The Bible refers to me as a shepherd. People are like sheep. As a pastor, I am always trying to gather people, lead and minister to people, understand people, and unlock people's lives. I am always studying people; learning people. I'm always trying to understand what makes them motivated and inspired. What matters to them?

"Behold, take notice, and pay attention." Pay attention to the proud. There's just something not right in the soul of a prideful person. Pride is a vice. Pride is a problem that comes from our inner person. The Bible says in Mark chapter 7 that it's what comes out of us that defiles our lives.

Our biggest problem isn't what is happening to us, it's what's happening *in* us. We defile ourselves by what comes out of us. Mark 7 also lists thirteen different vices. One of those is pride. Pride is a vice that comes out of us, that has the ability to sabotage our lives. That passage says, "Behold, their soul is not right." Pride is this arrogance that becomes insolence. You can't teach a prideful soul: it's defiant.

There's a certain disdain about pride. Pride lifts its nose, lifts its eyes, and looks down on other people. *You don't have any money, so I look down on you. You're struggling with an addiction, so I look down on you. You have a different color of skin, so I look down on you. You don't belong to the right whatever, so I look down on you. You don't have the right education, so I look down on you.* Pride is this disdain of others that looks down on people.

Pride invites violence into your life. Pride looks for a fight. Proverbs chapter 18:6 says, "A fool's words get them into constant quarrels." Let me ask you this: if you are always arguing with people, can you say fool? *I'm not the fool, everybody else is the fool!* We got it. You're not the problem; everybody else is the problem. The people you work with are the problem. The people you live with are the problem. Your neighbors are the problem. The people at the store are the problem. The people at the movie theater are the problem. They're all the problem.

Fools get into constant quarrels. Fools are asking for a beating. Because you cannot talk sense into them, you sometimes want to beat sense into them instead! God resists prideful attitudes. If God could talk sense into us and reach us with the spoken word, we would humble ourselves and change. But because He can't reach us with the spoken word, He has to discipline us. The Bible says those the Lord loves those He disciplines.

Maybe your spouse is not your problem. Maybe your pride is. Maybe your parents are not your problem. Your pride is. Maybe your boss or your company is not your problem, but your pride *is*. Maybe it's not the way people do church, because you're in the fifth church and none of them seem to do it right. Maybe it's not the church that's the problem. Maybe it's your pride. If you're constantly in relationship quarrels, you might be dealing with this issue of pride and foolishness. You're in danger of either devastating yourself, or at least embarrassing yourself.

In the next verse, Proverbs 26:11, it states, "As a dog returns to its own vomit, so a fool repeats his folly." That is disgusting and super embarrassing! This is exactly how craziness works. The dog vomits, he starts walking away and he thinks, *you know, that wasn't so bad. I'm going back for seconds.*

That's the way some people are. They're on the crazy train. They're on the Ozzie Osborn crazy train — the cycle of crazy — so they go over here and they vomit everywhere and blow their life up. They start walking away from crazy for a couple of minutes, and say, *you know, I think I'll go back and have seconds.*

You start coming to church for a couple of weeks, and you think, *uh, I don't know if I can live sane. This is not crazy enough, I think I'll go back to crazy.* Then you go back to crazy for another six months. *Oh, this is killing me. I'm more poor, I'm more broke, I'm more devastated and in more pain than I've ever been. I'm going to go back to church.* Now you make it for three weeks in a row. *Okay. I'm going to do better. I'm going to get right with God. Wait, this is not crazy. I don't know how to not do crazy. I don't know how to do normal. I don't know how to live without a fight. I don't know how to live without sabotage. I've just got to go back to crazy one more time.*

People go back to their mess and somehow think that's a good meal! They go back to crazy and think that's a good idea! We get out. We go back. We get out. We go back. Break the cycle of crazy! Pride will keep you in craziness.

Let me say it like this. Gentlemen, if calling your wife an idiot did not work the first time, it certainly won't work the second time. If you are still paying off last year's Christmas on your credit card, it's not a good idea to do it again this year. Do not go back and feed from that troubled trough again. If you do not have the money to buy them a gift, write them a poem. Call their cell phone and sing them a song. Draw a picture. Give them what you *do* have, not what you *don't* have. You do not ever have to go back.

You may be mad at me right now because you recently went and charged a bunch of stuff. But, you're probably still paying for gifts that somebody's already re-gifted to somebody else, or gave away at a white-elephant Christmas party somewhere! You're still paying for it and it's lost out there in give-away land. And then there's the interest charges. When you open your credit card bill in January, you're either going to say, "Oh, thank You God. I chose wisdom and I feel good today," or, a verse will start coming to your mind. *As a dog returns to its vomit, so does the Christmas spender who can't afford it.*

Christmas gift buying is a serious example. The reason some people can't tithe 10% is because they're paying 18% on credit card debt, on stuff that's long since been gone, without realizing that not tithing results in God withholding His shower of opportunity and blessing. You've got double trouble.

Proverbs 11:2 says, "When pride comes, shame is on its way." Which comes first? Pride, then shame. Pride means to not be restrained. When Adam and Eve were in the garden, the original sin was the lust of the flesh, the lust of the eye, and the pride of life. Can you imagine, they're in the perfect garden and have everything they want. They've got everything they need: a relationship with God, a purpose, they're naming the animals, a beautiful marriage...life is good.

God says, "Don't touch My tree." What do they want? They want the *only* thing God told them to stay away from. They did not practice restraint. They knowingly crossed God's boundaries. When God said, "Adam, where are you?" "I hid because I was naked. I was ashamed. It's Your fault, God, because You gave me that woman." See, this is all crazy. When we get into shame, we start justifying and blaming because of the embarrassment.

Proverbs 16:18 says, "Pride goes before destruction, and a haughty spirit before a fall." Have you ever dealt with someone with a haughty spirit? Was it your children? Have you ever noticed how teenagers can sometimes get that attitude that says, *my parents are morons? My parents are idiots. My parents are buffoons.* Now, this is coming from a person who can't afford a car, and if we let them live on their own, they would starve. Right? Also, their underwear would be so nasty because they don't know how to wash it. But, *my parents are idiots!*

Hmm, try doing life on your own and see how that works…

What it's saying is a haughty spirit goes before a fall. That means that someone's attitude is so elevated that they look down on others. It's no wonder a haughty spirit goes before a fall, because their nose is so far up in the air, they can't see where they're going or what they're tripping over.

The cure for the tattoo of foolishness and pride is humility. In Proverbs chapter 18, we read, "Pride first, then the crash. But humility is a pre-cursor to honor." I love that. God is saying, "Dave, if you'll humble yourself, it's a pre-cursor to honor." Do you understand how to be humble? Let me give you some keys:

Key #1: Humility is a position.
Humility means to lower yourself. It means to take a different position. It means to get at a level where you won't be *over* people, but at an eye-level *with* people. Jesus humbled Himself, got off of His throne, and got at our level. As a pastor, I'm always around children. I find if I lower myself, children are less intimidated. When you lower yourself to a child, you're saying they matter; they're important. This humility practices empathy.

Take time to listen to somebody else's story, not just talk about yours. When you lower yourself in position, you're saying to the other person, *you're important.* Humble people have the best relationships, because they *show* other people that they matter. That's exactly what Jesus did. Even when we were sinners, He stepped out of heaven, humbled Himself to be a friend to our destiny, because we matter to Him.

Key #2: Humility receives correction.
Pride resists correction. Humility says teach me, I don't know, or I don't understand.

Key #3: Humility is patience.
We get ourselves in trouble when we are impatient. Our decisions are rash, and sometimes our words are rash, too. Ecclesiastes chapter 7:8 says, "Finishing is better than starting, and patience is better than pride." If we will stay steady, we will reap success. Be consistent. Stay at it. "Be not weary," the Bible says, "for in due season you shall reap, if you faint not."

Key #4: Humility chooses right relationships.
Jesus says, "Come unto Me. My yoke is easy and my burden is light." Sometimes our breakthrough is just a step away from the right relationship.

These five keys aren't always easy, however, if we choose to practice them, we'll move through difficult situations much more easily! In fact, in living by these keys, foolish situations may actually occur a lot less frequently, too.

# CONCLUSION

'"Come now, and let us reason together,' says the Lord, 'Though your sins are like scarlet, they shall be as white as snow; though they are red like crimson, they shall be as wool.'" – Isaiah 1:18

Imagine all your heart's painful tattoos. Now imagine them washed away, replaced by something exceedingly beautiful; by something of heaven. The Master Artist's touch is evident in all His work.

Allow the walls of betrayal, embarrassment, and shame to fall before God, so He can come in and do a new work within you. If you let Him continue working on the lining of your heart, on the inner person of your spirit, and on the inner person of your being, your relationship with Him will change the direction of your life.

God loves to make all things new. Your Father does not want you live a heavy, bogged-down life any longer. He wants you to have the freedom of His presence, the freedom of His peace, and the nightmare tattoos replaced with His love and grace.

May you seek God's face and allow His hand to make all things new within your heart and mind.

"Create in me a clean heart, O God, and renew a steadfast spirit within me." – Psalm 51:10

PRAYER

Having a relationship with God starts with repentance. Maybe you don't have a relationship with God yet. The Bible says, we must be born again to have a relationship with Him. Maybe you need to reconnect to your relationship with God. Things got going with Him at one point, but life got busy. Something happened, and your relationship with God got disconnected. Pray this out loud:

"Father, today I open my heart and mind to You. I ask You to forgive me of my sins. Help me forgive those who've sinned against me. I ask you to be Lord and Savior from this day forward. I look to You for leadership in my life. I put my trust in You. In Jesus' Name."

When you prayed that, that's an apology and a prayer of new beginnings. If you prayed that prayer, I want to encourage you to start reading the Bible. Start talking to God every day. Start coming to church every week. Honor God with your time, and He will meet you there.

For additional copies of *Rebranded* for friends, family, Bible study groups, and military service members, please visit www.go2ccc.org or www.CreativeForcePress.com

Readers, if you've enjoyed this book, would you consider rating it and reviewing it on Amazon.com? Thank you.

About the Author

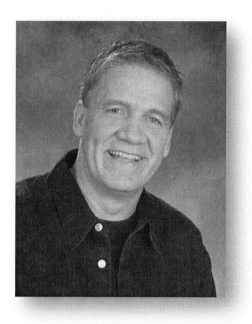

Pastor Dave Minton has been the senior pastor of Capital Christian Center (CCC) in Olympia, Washington, since 1988. Passionate about serving his community, local military personnel and ministry leaders, under the stewardship of Pastor Dave, CCC hosts free community outreach events, military fellowship ministry, celebrate recovery, leadership seminars, Formation school for ministry interns, ministries for children, youth, women and men, and offers more than eight services each week. Pastor Dave is married to Kelly, and together they have five grown children and two grandchildren.

www.go2ccc.org

REBRANDED is proudly published by:

Creative Force Press
Guiding Aspiring Authors to Release Their Dream

www.CreativeForcePress.com

Do You Have a Book in You?